GOD
is
GOOD

INTERACTIVE MANUAL

BILL JOHNSON

DESTINY IMAGE® PUBLISHERS, INC.

P.O. Box 310, Shippensburg, PA 17257-0310

"Promoting Inspired Lives."

This book and all other Destiny Image and Destiny Image Fiction books are available at Christian bookstores and distributors worldwide.

Cover design by Christian Rafetto
Interior design by Terry Clifton

For more information on foreign distributors, call 717-532-3040.

Reach us on the Internet: www.destinyimage.com.

ISBN 13 TP: 978-0-7684-1036-5
ISBN 13 eBook: 978-07684-1055-6

For Worldwide Distribution, Printed in the U.S.A.

1 2 3 4 5 6 7 8 / 20 19 18 17 16

He's better than we think.
So we need to change the way we think.
—BILL JOHNSON

CONTENTS

USING THE INTERACTIVE MANUAL

This interactive manual provides you with eight interactive sessions that you will go through together as a group or class. You may also engage the sessions individually, but you will get the most out of the curriculum content by engaging the sessions in a small group or class experience.

There is ample space for note-taking while going through the video sessions. Ask the Holy Spirit to highlight certain truths that are particularly relevant and applicable for your life while watching the teachings from Pastor Bill.

You will also have a listing of the different *Group Discussion Questions* and *Activation Exercises* that will be engaged after you watch the video session.

Additionally, you will have five daily reinforcement exercises. These are not intended to give you spiritual busywork, adding to what you are already doing in your walk with God. Rather, they function ideally as a themed, focused Bible study that will help you meditate on and start practicing what you learn during the weekly sessions. In order to strengthen yourself in the Lord, you need reinforcement. The keys that Bill Johnson provides in both the book and curriculum materials are designed for practical application.

In the daily readings and exercises you will engage the questions that follow each of the entries. As you engage each of the exercises, yielded to the Holy Spirit's direction and dependent upon His instruction, you will move from "glory to glory" in your relationship with the Lord and will be transformed into a growing disciple who learns how to live anchored in the goodness of God every day.

Following the daily readings, there are *Reflection Questions* for your interaction and *Prayers, Declarations, Meditations,* and *Reminders* that will help you personalize and seal the truths you learned.

GOD'S GOODNESS SHAPES OUR REALITY

*God's goodness is beyond our ability to comprehend,
but not our ability to experience.
Our hearts will take us where our heads can't fit.
Understanding is vital, but it often comes through experiencing God.*

NOTES ON SESSION 1

_____
_____
_____
_____
_____
_____
_____
_____
_____
_____
_____

> **We will always reflect the nature of the world that we are most aware of.**

_____
_____
_____
_____
_____
_____
_____
_____
_____

❝ *The hope of the world is not the return of the Lord; that's the hope of the Church.*

❝ *The hope of the world is the power of the Gospel.*

_____
_____
_____
_____
_____
_____
_____
_____
_____
_____
_____

> ❝ *You know your mind is renewed when the impossible looks logical.*

_____
_____
_____
_____
_____
_____
_____
_____
_____
_____
_____
_____
_____
_____
_____

> ❝ *Every revelation of God's nature is an invitation to encounter.*

_____
_____

> *Allow what God shows you to have greater weight in your life than the thousand questions you're asking.*

DISCUSSION QUESTIONS

1. Read Psalm 34:8. How does tasting the goodness of God change the way you see and interact with the world around you?

    a. Discuss. What do you think it looks like to taste and see that the Lord is good?

2. How does what you see of God actually change your countenance?

    a. Why is this important and how does your countenance represent the Lord?

    b. Is it possible for your countenance to pick up on the darkness and chaos around you?

3. Read Romans 12:1-2. How does a renewed or transformed mind impact the way you see God as good?

4. Read Matthew 6:10 and John 10:10. How do these Scriptures answer the question: What is the will of God?

5. Discuss and reflect on Pastor Bill's statement, "The hope of the world is not the return of the Lord; that's the hope of the Church. The hope of the world is the power of the Gospel."

6. Discuss: what does it mean to approve the will of God?

7. Discuss the Van Gogh illustration. How does this illustration show you how to approve the will of God?

    a. How does this illustration help you identify the work of God versus recognizing the work of the enemy?

8. Why is it so important that you have clarity on what comes from God and what comes from the enemy?

9. How do things change when you have it settled in your heart that God is good? (Specifically, how do you think your prayer life changes when you are convinced that God is good?)

ACTIVATION EXERCISE: RELEASE THE GOOD WILL OF GOD THROUGH PRAYER

The goal of today's session was to recalibrate how you think and how you live. One of the most fundamental activities of a Christian is prayer. This is not simply asking God for something; it's interacting with God. It's your dialogue with the Father. If your heart is not grounded in His goodness, you will come to Him with hesitation. Fear. Maybe shame and guilt. You will not pray boldly, expecting breakthrough.

It's time to change our perspective on God's goodness and start praying His *good will* over every situation and struggle we're facing.

Scripture makes it clear that God's will is to heal the sick, deliver the tormented, and save the lost. John 10:10 reminds that the thief (satan) came to steal, kill, and destroy; Jesus came to bring life and actually destroy the works of the devil. It's time to partner with the will of God by praying His purposes over every situation that is out of alignment with His good plan.

FAITH IN ACTION

Break up into prayer partners (groups of two work best—men with men and women with women, if possible). Share prayer needs/requests with each other. Before you start praying, *pray for each other's needs as if God is really good.*

Begin each prayer with declarations of God's goodness rather than going right into asking and petitioning. This approach will dramatically shift the way you pray for one another, focusing first and foremost on God's goodness. His goodness will set the standard for the kinds of prayers that will be prayed.

GOD'S GOODNESS SHAPES YOUR OUTLOOK

What comes into our minds when we think about God
is the most important thing about us.
—A.W. TOZER

If I were to do to my children what many people think God does to His children, I'd be arrested for child abuse. People say God is good, yet they credit Him with causing cancer and natural disasters and even blame Him for terrorist activities. Some try to escape the pain of such shameful reasoning by stating, "He allowed it" instead of "He caused it." In my way of thinking, there's little to no difference. If I abuse my children, or "allow/approve" a neighbor to do it, it's obvious I have a very serious problem. And when we sweep the abusive misdeed under the carpet called *God works in mysterious ways,* we add insult to injury. There is a common thought among many that God causes or allows evil to take place so He can display His mercy. That would be like me breaking my child's arm to show my ability to give him comfort, and then using my skills to reset the broken bone. People ask me, "What about Job?" My response is, "What about Jesus?" Job provides the question. Jesus gives the answer. The story of Job is about holding to our faith in the midst of trials and seeing God restore everything brilliantly. But the story of Jesus is the only one I follow.

There's no question that God can turn any situation around for His glory and for our benefit—this of course includes the most evil conditions known to humanity around the world. But that is the testimony of His greatness and His redemptive purpose. It does not represent His design. To attribute evil to Him tragically undermines our purpose on the earth, as it cripples our ability to *re*-present Jesus as the manifestation of God's *goodwill toward men.*

Our boldness to declare and demonstrate who He is in a given situation is seriously impaired if we're not confident of what He is like. When the boldness that is normal to the one filled with the Spirit of God diminishes, it costs us dearly. It is often our boldness that draws Him into an impossible situation.

QUESTIONS FOR REFLECTION

1. How is saying "God allowed it" similar to blaming God for causing the horrors in this world?

    _____

    _____

    _____

    _____

    _____

    _____

2. Why is it so important for us to have a biblical view of God's goodness? How do you think this impacts the way you represent Jesus in your everyday life?

    _____

    _____

    _____

    _____

    _____

    _____

3. Explain what you think life would look like if you were absolutely convinced that God was good? How would this shape the way you prayed?

    _____

    _____

    _____

    _____

    _____

    _____

PRAYER TO BEHOLD GOD'S GOODNESS

God, fill my eyes with a revelation of Your goodness! Help me to taste and see that You are good—and may that truth powerfully impact the way I represent Jesus in my everyday life. I declare, right now, that You are good. You're truly a good Father.

What's God? What's the Devil? How Can I Know the Difference?

The thief comes only to steal and kill and destroy; I came that they
may have life, and have it abundantly. I am the good shepherd;
the good shepherd lays down His life for the sheep.
—JOHN 10:10-11 NASB

It's not complicated. Loss, death, and destruction are the things left behind when the devil has had influence in a given situation. Jesus is the *Good* Shepherd. And what does that goodness look like? He gives abundant life. Here is it—loss, death, and destruction vs. abundant life. One is bad; the other is good. It shouldn't be that hard to distinguish between the two. And if that wasn't enough, John summarized why Jesus came to earth: *"The Son of God appeared for this purpose, to destroy the works of the devil"* (1 John 3:8 NASB). Jesus taught us how to recognize the works of the devil and then modeled how we destroy them. Do we have the right to set a new way of life and ministry that doesn't do what Jesus commanded us to do? No. Absolutely not!

It is time to reexamine our belief system and find out what the Bible really teaches about the nature of God. It really comes down to this—many have rejected the clear revelation of the nature of God that is seen in the person of Jesus Christ.

QUESTIONS FOR REFLECTION

1. Meditate on John 10:10. How does this passage of Scripture help you identify what comes from God and what comes from the devil (the thief)?

_____
_____
_____
_____
_____
_____
_____
_____

2. Based on First John 3:8, what should be the believer's response to the works of darkness?

_____
_____
_____
_____
_____
_____
_____
_____
_____
_____
_____
_____
_____

DECLARATION

I declare that You are good. You are the Author of life, Jesus! You came to set captives free, deliver the oppressed, heal the sick, and bring relief to the tormented. Thank You for wisdom to discern when You are at work and when the enemy is at work. Right now, I declare that I will be more mindful of what You are doing, Father, than what the enemy is doing. I will release Your goodness into every hopeless and dark situation, expecting that the thief will be driven out as the Kingdom of God is released in power.

THE RESPONSIBILITY TO CARRY GOD'S GOODNESS

Most assuredly, I say to you, he who believes in Me, the works that I do he will do also; and greater works than these he will do, because I go to My Father.
—JOHN 14:12

Most every believer confesses that God is good. We have to. It's in the Bible. It's not the belief in His goodness that threatens us. It's our definition of this goodness that has brought much debate and sometimes conflict and turmoil into the family of God.

If He is as good as many claim, how we respond to this truth will require massive change in how we do life. Instead of creating doctrines that explain away our weakness and anemic faith, we'll actually have to find out why *"the greater works than these"* have not been happening in and around us (see John 14:12). Creating doctrines of *no miracles today* not only contradicts His Word, it is a sneaky way to avoid responsibility. Instead of changing the standard for life given by Jesus, who walked the earth two thousand years ago, we are to embrace it and follow His model. We were designed with the capacity to be conformed into the likeness of Jesus, the One who is resurrected from the dead and is seated at the right hand of the Father (see 1 John 4:17).

The bottom line is, it was never meant that the hour we live in was to be inferior to Jesus' earthly ministry. John 14:12 is our invitation to embrace the opposite.

QUESTIONS FOR REFLECTION

1. Reflect and mediate on Jesus' words in John 14:12. How does your understanding of God's goodness determine what you do with this promise from Jesus?

_____
_____
_____
_____
_____
_____
_____
_____

2.   The common response to scriptures like John 14:12 is "this is not happening so it must not be true," or "that promise is not for believers today." Based on the devotional reading today, how do you think Jesus wants you to pray promises like this?

_____
_____
_____
_____
_____
_____
_____
_____
_____
_____

PRAYER INVITATION

The Holy Spirit is calling you to take ownership over promises like John 14:12 and pray them. Take a moment right now to recognize what the Lord wants to do—He is calling you, His son, His daughter, into a unique partnership with Heaven. God's will is made known to you for the purpose of calling you into partnership. John 14:12 is an expression of His will. Heaven desires for the Father's agenda to be released on earth; however, the Lord is looking for those on earth who will faithfully believe that Heaven's promises and purposes are for right now!

Simply pray:

Lord, I say "Yes." I say "Yes" to both the same works as Jesus and the "greater works" He promised.

EXPERIENCING GOD'S GOODNESS IS THE KEY TO TRUE UNDERSTANDING

Taste and see that the Lord is good.
—PSALM 34:8 NASB

God's goodness is beyond our ability to comprehend, but not our ability to experience. Our hearts will take us where our heads can't fit. Understanding is vital, but it often comes through experiencing God. Faith for the journey of walking with God leads to encounters with God. It results in a growing knowledge and understanding of truth, as in *"by faith we understand that the worlds were framed by the word of God"* (Heb. 11:3). Having said that, one of the great commands of Scripture pertaining to the experience of His goodness is *"taste and see that the Lord is good"* (Ps. 34:8). If you'll *taste it* for yourself, you'll *see it* more clearly. Your perception of truth will increase as you experience truth more deeply.

As it is with this most important doctrine of *being born again*, we always understand a subject more clearly once we've experienced it. Hearing someone teach on being born again who isn't born again is almost laughable. There is hardly a group of believers anywhere that would treasure that teaching. Yet a similar practice is almost applauded as noble in much of Christendom—theology that requires no experience. I realize that some may assume I mean that theology is based on experience, which implies to some we throw reason out the door. That is a true and present danger. But the issue that has had much more damage in present-day church life is theology without experience. The Pharisees were known for theories that never had an effect on their own lives. To combat this, we must exercise our faith to put a demand on what we believe.

QUESTIONS FOR REFLECTION

1. How can you experience God's goodness without completely understanding it?

_____

_____

_____

_____

_____

2. Describe some ways that you have personally "tasted and seen" that God is good. It's important to keep these testimonies close to you, remembering them often. More than being answered prayers, miracles, and breakthroughs, these all say something very clear about the goodness of God. As you reflect on a few key moments in your life where God showed you—visibly—that He was good, be sure to write down what that moment reveals about God's character.

_____

_____

_____

_____

_____

_____

_____

_____

_____

_____

_____

_____

_____

PRAYER TO EXPERIENCE GOD'S GOODNESS

Father, You are inviting me into an encounter with Your goodness. I say, "Yes, Lord!" Right now, I recognize that even though Your goodness is beyond my understanding, it is not beyond my ability to experience. So here I am, Lord! Mark my life by Your goodness. Shift the way I think because my mind is under the influence of Your goodness. May every area of how I live my life be shaped and reshaped by the fact that You are good!
Come, Holy Spirit, and immerse me in the Father's goodness—even now.

Day Five

Your Gateway to Encounter God's Goodness: The Renewed Mind

*And do not be conformed to this world, but be transformed by
the renewing of your mind, so that you may prove what the will
of God is, that which is good and acceptable and perfect.*
—ROMANS 12:2

The renewed mind is more than having the ability to give a biblical answer to a problem. It includes that, but in reality it is so much more. It is seeing from a divine perspective.

In the Romans passage, the renewed mind proves the will of God. That is fascinating when you realize that the best definition for the will of God in Scripture is *"Your will be done, on earth as it is in heaven"* (Matt. 6:10). It can be said that the renewed mind is what reveals and illustrates God's will on earth. The mind of Christ, seen in Jesus' lifestyle, illustrates this beautifully. He confronted storms, healed bodies, multiplied food, and did countless other miracles to reveal Heaven's effect on earth. The renewed mind in us should do the same. We will know our mind is renewed when the impossible looks logical.

QUESTIONS FOR REFLECTION

1. What do you think it means to "see from divine perspective"? How does this relate to seeing your current situation in light of God's goodness?

2.   How does the renewed mind approve the will of God? Explain how you can take the Van Gogh illustration (from this week's video session) and apply it to situations that you or others are confused about.

_____
_____
_____
_____
_____
_____
_____

3.   How does "approving" God's will in a situation give you clear direction on how to pray (when you have a clear view of what God's heart is on the matter you're praying about)?

_____
_____
_____
_____
_____
_____
_____
_____

PRAYER FOR THE RENEWAL OF YOUR MIND

Father, I ask You to change the way I think.
Any area of my thinking that is not influenced by Your goodness, I ask you to transform.
Right now, I simply wait in Your Presence.
I thank You that as I spend time with You, You change the way I think.
As I study Your Word, Holy Spirit, You wash and cleanse my mind.
Help me approve Your will, Lord.
May my thinking be under the influence of Your goodness!

God's Goodness Is Defined in His Original Design for Creation

Discovering God's original commission and purpose for mankind can help to fortify our resolve to a life of history-shaping significance. To find that truth, we must go back to the beginning.

NOTES ON SESSION 2

> *God won't share His glory with another...but you're not "another."*

> **Jesus gives us all the authority to complete His assignment.**

_____
_____
_____
_____
_____

> **Eternity is the cornerstone of all logic and reason.**

_____
_____
_____
_____
_____
_____
_____
_____
_____
_____
_____
_____
_____
_____
_____
_____
_____
_____
_____
_____
_____

> **You can tell how much God trusts you by looking at what He entrusted to you.**

_____
_____

> **What did He entrust to you? The Holy Spirit.**

DISCUSSION QUESTIONS

1. Read Romans 3:23. What was the original realm that mankind was supposed to live in? Discuss what you think this looked like in Eden.

   a. Describe how Jesus restored mankind to the place of glory.

2. Reflect on Genesis 1. How does the original design represent God's perfect and good will? What language might confirm this?

3. What is mankind's job in representing God's goodness and reign in the world today—just like in Eden?

4. Read Genesis 1:26–28. How did the mandate for mankind to expand the Garden of Eden (through Adam and Eve) actually reveal His will for the world throughout all of time?

5. Why did God create options and how does this reveal His goodness (starting with the option for Adam and Eve to eat of the forbidden fruit)?

6. Read Luke 4:6 and Luke 19:10. When Jesus talks about seeking and saving "that which was lost," discuss the fullness of what He is talking about.

7. Explain your understanding of God's keys of authority—how were they taken away and how were they given back?

8. Explain Pastor Bill's comment, "You were born into a war zone." Why is it important to live mindful of this conflict without being too focused on the powers of darkness?

   a. How does your understanding of this war zone give perspective on the surrounding situations, chaos, and crisis in the world?

9. How does your understanding of God's original design for creation (before sin and the Fall) give you a clear blueprint for His will?

   a. How does your understanding of God's good design give you a filter to see life through?

ACTIVATION EXERCISE: RELEASE THE AUTHORITY OF GOD

The goal of today's session was to give you a clear blueprint of God's good design and intent for creation. As seen in Luke 4:6, keys of authority were given to the devil in the Fall of mankind, giving him influence over affairs and activities on planet Earth. Though the devil is not sovereign by any stretch, he was still given access to influence situations and people in the world. Jesus came to *seek and save that which was lost*—lost people, yes, but also lost keys of authority.

Because *all authority* was given to Jesus and then Jesus commissioned His people to complete *His* task, it's safe to say that the One who was given all authority has entrusted *you* with His authority!

FAITH IN ACTION

Pastor Bill gave the example of Isaiah 66:8, where the question is asked: *Can a nation be saved in a day?* God is extending an invitation to His commissioned people to actually bring Him the fruit of a *nation saved in a day*. We have been authorized to fulfill the commission of Jesus; this is why He gave us authority to disciple the nations (see Matt. 28).

Here are some prayer directives:

1. Pray as a group for the commission of Jesus to be accomplished through each person present.

    a. Pray for the harvest of nations to be brought in.

    b. Pray for a release of signs, wonders, and miracles throughout the global church—an outpouring of the supernatural that will usher the masses into the Kingdom of God.

    c. Pray for cities, regions, and nations to be impacted by the Presence and power of God.

2. Pray for the Holy Spirit to release vision and clarity on the unique ways that He wants to activate the people to fulfill this commission. (Note: it's not simply through church work and "full-time ministry." God has an assignment for every single person, with each assignment being equal in value, regardless of what sphere of influence that person is placed in.)

3. Pray that each person has a revelation of the "sacredness" of his or her calling. In these final moments, you can break up into smaller groups and pray for/prophesy over each other. Specifically, have the prayer focus be on activating each other to fulfill God's commission and release His power in their unique spheres of influence.

A Clear Blueprint of God's Goodness

You will know the truth, and the truth will make you free.
—JOHN 8:32 NASB

Because God is better than I think, I must adjust my thinking and the tenderness of my heart until I live conscious of both His nature and His Presence. And that awareness then becomes the reality I live from. His nature defines who I am and what I do. This greatest reality of all realities is to become my spiritual, emotional, and intellectual home. In the same way I travel from my home to my office, or from my home to minister in another country, so His nature is to become the home I travel from—it is the reference point for all of life. And though I travel great distances from my home, I am never to be away from the awareness of His goodness. That is the home or the abiding place of my heart that goes with me everywhere.

He longs to reveal Himself to those who are ready to fully embrace what they discover. In many ways our *yes* precedes seeing more of Him. Our *yes* is our invitation for more of Him. Revelation of truth releases responsibility for truth. Revelation is seldom given to those who are merely curious. You'll never see Him reveal truth just to make us smarter or more capable of debating with those who see differently. Truth by nature is the transforming power of God to instill freedom in the life of those who embrace it. It could be said that freedom exists in a person's life to the degree he embraces truth from the heart. It's more than a mental agreement to a concept called truth. It is the heartfelt *yes* to a way of life. That way of life becomes measureable in our lifestyle of freedom. Jesus put it this way: *"You will know the truth, and the truth will make you free"* (John 8:32 NASB). My journey starts to break down when my thoughts violate who He is. When our questions express our hunger for discovery, they're fruitful. But when our questions challenge who He is, they are foolish and lead to intellectual pride and ultimately spiritual barrenness.

Who He is is revealed in what He says. He identifies Himself as the Word. In other words, He says nothing apart from who He is. His Word reveals His nature and manifests His Presence. Jesus was never a broadcaster of truths He didn't live. Even the people of His day recognized this as a reason for His unequalled authority—*"Never has a man spoken the way this man speaks"* (John 7:46 NASB).

QUESTIONS FOR REFLECTION

1. How does the Word (the Bible and the person of Jesus) give you a clear blueprint of what God's goodness looks like?

    _____

    _____

    _____

    _____

    _____

    _____

    _____

    _____

    _____

    _____

    _____

    _____

2. Reflect on John 8:32. How does your revelation and understanding of God's truth actually determine the level of freedom you enjoy?

    _____

    _____

    _____

    _____

    _____

    _____

    _____

    _____

    _____

    _____

    _____

PRAYER FOR FREEDOM THROUGH REVELATION

God, I am on a journey of discovery.

I want to discover the truth about Your goodness, so I can enjoy the freedom You've made available.

Open my eyes in new ways.

I pray that in the days to come, I would receive a very clear understanding of what Your original will and purpose was for creation.

Jesus, You came to seek and save that which was lost.

I pray that in the readings to come, You would show me what was lost, how Jesus got it back, and how You have commissioned me to use Your keys of authority today!

REDISCOVERING GOD'S ORIGINAL COMMISSION

*Then God said, "Let Us make man in Our image, according to Our likeness;
let them have dominion over the fish of the sea, over the birds of the
air, and over the cattle, over all the earth and over every creeping thing
that creeps on the earth." So God created man in His own image; in the
image of God He created him; male and female He created them. Then
God blessed them, and God said to them, "Be fruitful and multiply; fill
the earth and subdue it; have dominion over the fish of the sea, over the
birds of the air, and over every living thing that moves on the earth."*
—GENESIS 1:26–28

Man was created in the image of God and placed into the Father's ultimate expression of beauty and peace—the Garden of Eden. Outside of that garden, it was a different story. It was without the order and blessing contained within and was in great need of the touch of God's delegated one—Adam. It's an amazing thought to consider that something could be so perfect and good from God's perspective, yet be incomplete. God Himself longed to see what those who worshiped by choice would do with what He gave them to steward.

Adam and Eve were placed in the Garden with a mission. God said, *"Be fruitful and multiply; fill the earth and subdue it"* (Gen. 1:28). This was the first commission given to mankind. *"Be fruitful."* This is a specific command to be productive. It included discovering the laws of God's creation and cooperating with them to make the ever-expanding Garden a better place. God was not afraid of their personalizing His creation. Their mark of delegated authority was to be seen in their management of creation itself.

"Multiply." They were to have children, who in turn would have children, etc. It was God's intention that as they bore more children, who also lived under God's rule, they would be able to extend the boundaries of His Garden through the simplicity of their devotion to Him. Because they were His delegated authority, they could display the beauty of God's Kingdom by representing Him well. The greater the number of people in right relationship to God, the greater the impact of their leadership. This process was to continue until the entire earth was covered with the glorious rule of God through man.

"Fill the earth." This statement reveals that God's target was the entire planet. One can only imagine what that might have looked like had Adam and Eve not sinned—humanity living in perfect harmony, under one God, all working to glorify God through their management of what He had created. Every corner of the earth was to feel the influence of His delegated ones, who served and ruled out of love—love for God, love for one another, and love for all that He had made.

"Subdue it." This statement reveals something that is often ignored. The Garden of Eden was perfect. But the rest of the planet was in disarray. Outside of the Garden was chaos and disorder as it was under the influence of the devil and his hordes. For that reason, a military term was used to describe Adam and Eve's assignment. In a sense they were born into a war. They were to bring the earth under their control and ultimately under the influence of God through their righteous rule.

Because satan had rebelled and had been cast out of Heaven with a portion of the fallen angels and had taken dominion of the earth, it becomes obvious why the rest of the planet needed to be subdued—it was under the influence of the powers of darkness. (See Genesis 1:2.) God could have destroyed the devil and his host with a word; instead He chose to defeat darkness through His delegated authority—those made in His image who were lovers of God by choice.

QUESTIONS FOR REFLECTION

1. Explain your understanding of how God's threefold mandate to multiply, fill the earth, and subdue it applies to your Christian life today.

2. What is revealed about God's goodness when He uses His delegated authority on earth—you and I—to defeat the powers of darkness?

PRAYER OF COMMISSIONING

Father, I ask for fresh clarity on my assignment as Your delegated authority.
Increase my confidence—not in myself, but in every resource You've equipped me with to complete the assignment You've given to me.
I thank You for Your Word.
Your Spirit.
Your authority.
Your approval.
Your promises.
Your power.
May I live more mindful of what You have entrusted to me than the lack or crisis I come against.

Day Eight

YOUR ASSIGNMENT TO RELEASE GOD'S GOODNESS ON EARTH

The heaven, even the heavens, are the Lord's; but the
earth He has given to the children of men.
—PSALM 115:16

The Sovereign One placed us—Adam's children—in charge of planet Earth, even though we were only capable of managing a small portion to start with. He did something similar to the children of Israel when He gave them all of the Promised Land. He basically told them, "It's all yours, although I'll give it to you little by little." He then went on to explain that the timing of the release of their inheritance was for their sake, so the beasts of the field wouldn't become too numerous for them. This is remarkable. From day one, God has longed for His people to rule out of their right relationship with Him. The centurion brilliantly illustrates this same principle when he asks Jesus to heal his servant in Matthew 8:7–10:

> *Jesus said to him, "I will come and heal him." But the centurion said, "Lord, I am not*
> *worthy for You to come under my roof, but just say the word, and my servant will be*
> *healed. For I also am a man under authority, with soldiers under me; and I say to this one,*
> *'Go!' and he goes, and to another, 'Come!' and he comes, and to my slave, 'Do this!' and*
> *he does it." Now when Jesus heard this, He marveled and said to those who were following,*
> *"Truly I say to you, I have not found such great faith with anyone in Israel"* (NASB).

Because the centurion was under authority, he knew he had authority. Adam and Eve were given a huge assignment, which depended on their relationship with God, not their gifts and talents alone. Their authority was based entirely on being under the authority of the Almighty God. God's mission is to be embraced and represented well by those who love Him by choice, bringing all that He has made back into its proper place.

"*The heaven, even the heavens, are the Lord's; but the earth He has given to the children of men*" (Ps. 115:16). This highest of honors was given to us because love always chooses the best. That is the beginning of the romance of our creation—created in His image, *for intimacy*, that dominion might be expressed through love. It is from this revelation that we are to learn to walk as His ambassadors, thus defeating the "prince of this world" (see John 14:30; Eph. 2:2). The stage was set for all of darkness to fall as man exercised his godly influence over creation. But instead, man fell.

QUESTIONS FOR REFLECTION

1.   Explain how God entrusts authority to His people, based on your devotional reading today.

_____

_____

_____

_____

_____

_____

_____

_____

_____

_____

_____

_____

2.   Explain how something can be all yours and yet you still need to receive it little by little. This is true with all of the promises of God. Even though we have received every one, by inheritance, what do you think the danger of receiving everything all at once would be?

_____

_____

_____

_____

_____

_____

_____

3. How does your assignment depend on intimacy with God (as opposed to your talent, abilities, opportunities, upbringing, etc.)?

PRAYER OF PERSPECTIVE

Father, I place myself under Your authority.

I submit to Your mission.

Your primary mission, God, is my commission.

Wherever You've put me, and with whatever You've given me, show me how to serve Your commission.

Above all, Lord, I remain connected to You.

My pleasure and delight is Your Presence.

I don't live for my assignment; I live for You!

I don't find my identity in my gifts or talents; I find my identity and purpose in You and what You say about me.

Show me how to release and demonstrate Your goodness on earth.

Day Nine

Understanding the Fall of Mankind

*Satan, who is the god of this world, has blinded
the minds of those who don't believe.*
—2 CORINTHIANS 4:4 NLT

Satan didn't come into the Garden of Eden and violently take possession of Adam and Eve. He couldn't—he had no dominion there. Dominion empowers. And because man was given the keys of dominion over the planet, the devil would have to get his authority from man. The suggestion to eat the forbidden fruit was simply the devil's effort to get Adam and Eve to agree with him in opposition to God, thus empowering him. To this day it is through agreement that the devil is able to *kill, steal, and destroy.* He is still empowered through man's agreement.

Mankind's authority to rule was forfeited when Adam ate the forbidden fruit. Paul said, *"You are that one's slaves whom you obey"* (Rom. 6:16). In that one act, mankind went from ruler over a planet to the slave and possession of the evil one. All that Adam owned, including the title deed to the planet with its corresponding position of rule, became part of the devil's spoil. God's predetermined plan of redemption immediately kicked into play: *"I will put enmity between you and the woman, and between your seed and her seed; he shall bruise your head, and you shall bruise His heel"* (Gen. 3:15). Jesus would come to reclaim all that was lost.

God's plan of rulership for man never ceased. Jesus came to bear man's penalty for sin and recapture what had been lost. Luke 19:10 records that Jesus came *"to seek and to save that which was lost."* Not only was mankind lost to sin, his dominion over planet Earth was also lost. Jesus came to recapture all that was lost.

QUESTIONS FOR REFLECTION

1. Based on the video session and this devotional reading, explain your understanding of: 1) how authority was given by God to Adam and Eve in the Garden of Eden; 2) how Adam and Eve, representing mankind, gave authority to satan through sin; and 3) the impact this authority exchange has had on the planet ever since.

_____
_____
_____
_____
_____
_____
_____
_____
_____
_____
_____
_____
_____
_____
_____
_____
_____
_____
_____
_____
_____
_____
_____
_____
_____

2. Read and reflect on Luke 19:10. Based on your understanding of what was given away in the Garden of Eden, list some of what you believe Jesus came to "seek and save."

_____
_____
_____

_____

_____

_____

_____

_____

_____

_____

_____

_____

_____

_____

_____

_____

_____

_____

_____

_____

_____

_____

_____

UNDERSTANDING THE AUTHORITY EXCHANGE: A NEW REVELATION OF GENESIS

It is absolutely essential that every Christian understands the exchange that took place in the Garden of Eden. Without this knowledge, it is impossible to effectively interact with the life situations we all face today.

Here is your charge today—read Genesis 1–3 and ask the Holy Spirit to give you a clear view of what creation was like *before* the introduction of sin and the influence of satan. This is a picture of the Creator's original intent and design.

Consider a junkyard filled with expensive European cars. Even though you presently see the vehicles in a state of absolute destruction and decay, that was not the manufacturer's original design for that vehicle. The same is true for what we see and experience in the world today.

JESUS RESTORED THE KEYS OF AUTHORITY

*So Jesus said to them again, "Peace to you! As the Father has sent
Me, I also send you." And when He had said this, He breathed
on them, and said to them, "Receive the Holy Spirit."*
—JOHN 20:21-22

In redeeming man, Jesus recovered what man had given away. From the throne of triumph He declared, *"All authority has been given to Me in heaven and on earth.* (Matt. 28:18). In other words: *I got the keys back. Now go use them and reclaim what was lost.* In this passage, Jesus fulfills the promise He made to the disciples when He said, *"I will give you the keys of the kingdom of heaven"* (Matt. 16:9). The original plan was never aborted; it was fully realized once and for all in the resurrection and ascension of Jesus. We were then to be completely restored to His plan of ruling as a people made in His image. And as such, we would learn how to enforce the victory obtained at Calvary: *"The God of peace will soon crush Satan under your feet"* (Rom. 16:19 NASB).

We were born to rule—rule over creation, over darkness—to plunder hell, to rescue those headed there, and to establish the rule of Jesus wherever we go by preaching the Gospel of the Kingdom. *Kingdom* means *King's domain, King's dominion.* In the original purpose of God, mankind ruled over creation. Now that sin has entered the world, creation has been infected by darkness, namely disease, sickness, afflicting spirits, poverty, natural disasters, demonic influence, etc. Our rule is still over creation, but now it is focused on exposing and undoing the works of the devil. We are to give what we have received to reach that end. (See Matthew 10:8.) If I truly receive power from an encounter with the God of power, I am equipped to give it away. The invasion of God into impossible situations comes through a people who have received power from on high and have learned to release it into the circumstances of life.

QUESTIONS FOR REFLECTION

1. What are some ways that you can demonstrate Jesus' Kingdom authority in the circumstances of life? (Remember John 20:21-22—the works that Jesus was commissioned to do, you are also commissioned to perform in His name.)

_____

_____

_____

_____

_____

_____

_____

_____

_____

_____

_____

_____

_____

_____

_____

_____

_____

_____

_____

2. Describe how the expressions of the Kingdom—healing, deliverance, demonstration of miracles, signs, and wonders—reveal the goodness of God as they are released?

_____

_____

_____

PRAYER OF EMPOWERMENT

Holy Spirit, I ask You to fall upon me right now in a fresh way.

Just like You empowered Jesus to do the supernatural works of the Kingdom, You've authorized and empowered me to do the same acts.

Miracles and healings.

Deliverance.

Signs and wonders.

Operating in prophecy, words of knowledge, discerning of spirits, and every gift of the Holy Spirit.

These are available to me.

They are free gifts.

I didn't earn them and I don't deserve them—Jesus did and Jesus won them for me.

Lord, as I freely receive, help me to freely give.

And as You release Your power in and through me, show the world a greater glimpse of Your goodness!

GOD'S GOODNESS REVEALED IN THE OLD TESTAMENT

The entire Old Testament points to Jesus. He is the central figure of all Scripture. Both the Law and the Prophets declared His role as Messiah, showing how Jesus would fulfill God's redemptive plan. The stories, prophecies, and laws all pointed to Him at various levels in the same way that a highway sign points to an upcoming city from varying distances.

NOTES ON SESSION 3

_____
_____
_____
_____
_____
_____
_____
_____
_____
_____
_____
_____
_____
_____
_____
_____

> *A person who doesn't believe in the authenticity of the Law is not going to believe in the authenticity of the Gospel.*

_____
_____
_____
_____
_____
_____
_____
_____
_____
_____

> **Find the everyones and find the alls in Scripture. They are truths that are so huge they tend to be read over quickly instead of adopted and embraced.**

DISCUSSION QUESTIONS

Discuss the four purposes of the Old Testament:

1. Reveal the severity of sin—explain how and why sin is so severe (see Ezek. 18:20).

2. Reveal the hopelessness of fallen humanity—discuss why it's so important to understand how hopeless and lost man was, in order to fully grasp the goodness of God through the work of Jesus.

3. Point to mankind's need for a Savior—how does the Old Testament testify of Christ?

4. Point to the coming of a Savior—discuss how different aspects of the Old Testament (like the Tabernacle of Moses) actually reveal Jesus.

5. Read Luke 16:16. Discuss Pastor Bill's statement: "The nature of the message (the Kingdom of God is at hand) determines the size of the harvest."
   a. Discuss what the Gospel of the Kingdom looks like as opposed to a Gospel of salvation. What does this include?
   b. How does the announcement of God's Kingdom have a direct impact on the size of the harvest of people who respond to it?

6. How should you respond to the alls and everyones in Scripture—those promises in the Bible that sound "too good to be true"? (List some examples of these kinds of promises.)

7. Explain how the cross of Jesus Christ has an impact on everything, specifically:
   a. What ended at the cross?
   b. What changed at the cross?
   c. What made it through the cross unchanged?

8. Discuss why it's important to read and study the Old Testament, even though we're under the New Covenant.

ACTIVATION EXERCISE: RETURN TO THE OLD TO DISCOVER THE NEW

The goal of today's session was to help you see the purpose of the Old Testament. Unfortunately, due to misunderstanding and lack of clear instruction, many simply reject what is written in the Old Testament, they fail to engage with it, or, worse, they are confused about the nature of God, thinking that He either changed or is inconsistent in nature. Even though every theological question about the transition between Old and New Covenants was not explored, some of the more pressing topics were addressed, and now you have been given a blueprint on how to start looking for God's goodness in the Old Testament.

FAITH IN ACTION: OLD COVENANT CHALLENGE

This week, intentionally spend time reading the Old Testament. This is your charge—*look for God's goodness.* Even in some of the more confusing and perhaps seemingly awkward parts of the Old Testament, ask the Holy Spirit to reveal God's goodness based on the criteria you learned from Pastor Bill. Before you leave the meeting, spend some time in group prayer. Ask the Holy Spirit:

- to come and reveal God's goodness using the pages of the Old Testament.

- to stir up a passion for the entire Bible, Old and New Testaments alike.

- to usher people into encounters with God using the Old Testament stories as entryways into His Presence.

- to provide practical, everyday instruction to God's people using the stories and principles in the Old Testament.

- to help you read the Old Testament clearly, applying the four purposes that Pastor Bill taught in the session.

THE OLD TESTAMENT REVEALS
SIN AS SEVERE AND DEADLY

*And you He made alive, who were dead in trespasses and sins, in which
you once walked according to the course of this world, according to
the prince of the power of the air, the spirit who now works in the sons
of disobedience, among whom also we all once conducted ourselves
in the lusts of our flesh, fulfilling the desires of the flesh and of the
mind, and were by nature children of wrath, just as the others.*
—EPHESIANS 2:1–3

Sin is so severe it is terminal in every single case. It cannot be overlooked. The presence and power of sin have scarred all that God has made. No one can survive the effects of sin. The apostle Paul explains the role of the Law as it pertains to sin: *"where there is no law there is no transgression"* (Rom. 4:15). God does nothing to create shame in us. All that He reveals to us He does out of His goodness so that we might respond to His provision and become free. Without knowing our need, it's impossible to recognize His answer. When He reveals our absolute lost condition because of sin, He does so that we might turn from sin and receive His solution—forgiveness unto adoption.

The Law drives this point home over and over again by illustrating how sin contaminates everything it touches. For example, if you touch a leper in the Old Testament, you are unclean, requiring a process to become clean again. If you are bringing a lamb to be sacrificed, and somebody spits on it, the offering is now unclean. The idea is driven home page after page as the severity of sin must be realized to effectively turn from it unto God. The point is, under the Old Covenant unclean things affect the clean things. Sin contaminates.

The Old Testament gives us an awareness of our sinfulness, revealing that we can't just decide not to sin anymore. It has become our nature. No amount of discipline or determination can change our bent toward sin, nor can it rid us of our sinful past. One of the more sobering realizations is that there is no number of good works that can make up for our sins. Self-help programs might help with losing weight or learning new skills. But they cannot touch the human dilemma called sin. It is out of the reach of all human efforts. Seeing that we are lost—completely lost—helps us to see our need of a savior.

Because sin contaminates all it touches, Israel had to destroy the surrounding nations when they entered the Promised Land. There was nothing put into place that could change the bent toward sin of the people who once occupied their inheritance. The only answer was their death; otherwise, their sinful nature would contaminate the work that God was doing in His own people. That's quite a difference from the Old Covenant to the New, where we are commanded to take this Good News to the surrounding nations and seek for their conversion.

QUESTIONS FOR REFLECTION

1. Why is it so important to understand the absolute severity of sin?

_____

_____

_____

_____

_____

_____

_____

_____

_____

_____

_____

_____

_____

_____

2. How does understanding the severity of sin help us appreciate the goodness of God?

_____

_____

_____

_____

_____

_____

_____

_____

_____

_____

_____

_____

_____

_____

_____

3. How did sin make the divine intervention of God absolutely necessary for salvation?

_____

_____

_____

_____

_____

_____

_____

_____

_____

_____

_____

_____

PRAYER OF REFLECTION

Lord, before Your grace came into my life, I was a hopeless, lost sinner.
Thank You for the work of Jesus.
By reading the Old Testament, I am confronted with how deadly sin is.
I pray that as I confront the reality of sin, I would also be overcome with thanksgiving for how glorious the cross of Jesus Christ truly is!

THE OLD TESTAMENT REVEALS MY NEED FOR A SAVIOR

*But God demonstrates His own love toward us, in that
while we were still sinners, Christ died for us.*
—ROMANS 5:8

Seeing that we are utterly lost helps to open us up to outside help. And that outside help is from God Himself. The stubborn insistence that we provide for ourselves and take care of ourselves might help in some parts of life. But that trait is completely useless as it pertains to our need of salvation. Because we are lost, we must be found. In reality, none of us can "find Jesus." The Bible describes us as dead (separate from God). And dead people can't find a savior. Strangely, this provides the backdrop for all of us, as it pertains to our salvation. Those who are seeking God are simply responding to the summons of God that has been released over their hearts. We were found. Jesus called us by name, bringing conviction of sin into our lives. We responded and were born again—we came to life.

The Old Testament Law is the teacher that leads us to Christ. It first reveals that we are sinners, but thankfully, it doesn't leave us there. *"Therefore the Law has become our tutor to lead us to Christ, so that we may be justified by faith. But now that faith has come, we are no longer under a tutor"* (Gal. 3:24-25 NASB). Jesus not only satisfied the appetite of the Law in bearing our judgment upon Himself; He was the One the Law was pointing to, much like a sign on a restaurant points to what's inside the building. The Mosaic Law pointed to Jesus. There are many wonderful books that help to identify how the sacrifices, the feasts, the furniture of the Tabernacle of Moses, the Sabbath and Jubilee, and countless other things point to the coming of Jesus. That doesn't even count the prophecies that specifically announce the details of His life and His death. It was clearly announced to help His people recognize Him when He came. Tragically, many of the ones who were the most trained in the study of Scripture missed Jesus when He came. Their increased knowledge insulated them from their own needs and didn't lead them to a tender heart.

As you read and reread Old Testament Scriptures, it becomes obvious that the Father wanted us to realize that His answer was on the way. The Savior was on the way.

QUESTIONS FOR REFLECTION

1. Describe how reading the Old Testament makes you aware of your need for a Savior.

    _____

    _____

    _____

    _____

    _____

    _____

    _____

    _____

2. Consider some of the different Old Testament stories you've read. Identify some where you can clearly see references to Jesus (like the Tabernacle that Pastor Bill described in the video session).

    _____

    _____

    _____

    _____

    _____

    _____

PRAYER OF PRAISE

Father, thank You for Jesus!
While I was still a sinner, not even looking for You, You came after me.
While I was living my own life, doing my own thing, You pursued me.
Even if I've known You most of my life, Lord, I know that You pursued my family.
You broke into past generations with Your mighty saving power.
You put people in my life who prayed for me to receive the work of Jesus.
God, apart from Your help, Your intervention, Your power, and Your invasion in my life, I would still be lost. I'd be in darkness, bound to sin.
Right now, I praise You for sending Jesus.

Take this time to simply express your praise and thanksgiving to God for the saving work of Jesus.

THE GOSPEL OF THE KINGDOM

The law and the prophets were until John. Since that time the kingdom
of God has been preached and everyone is pressing into it.
—LUKE 16:16

"*Until John*" is a very significant phrase, but one that seems to be mostly ignored. Both the Law and the Prophets were *trumped* by a greater message, the Gospel of the Kingdom. One is the prevailing message while the other is obsolete, having been fulfilled. One has Heaven's backing; the other doesn't. One reveals God's purpose in this present day, defining our assignment; the other does not.

A message creates a reality. The nature of the message we carry determines the nature of the reality we will live and minister in. Those who fully embrace our God-given assignment for the message of the Kingdom will see the ever-increasing government of God displayed in the affairs of mankind. This is the only message that creates an environment suitable to the display of God's love, His uncompromising purity, and His unfathomable power. This is the message that Jesus preached and in turn taught His disciples to preach. It remains the *now word*.

The Church has largely replaced the Gospel of the Kingdom with the Gospel of salvation. It's the beauty of the salvation message that makes it so easy to miss the fact that it is only a part of the whole message that Jesus gave us. The Gospel of salvation is focused on getting people saved and going to Heaven. The Gospel of the Kingdom is focused on the transformation of lives, cities, and nations through the effect of God's present rule—this is made manifest by bringing the reality of Heaven to earth. We must not confuse our destiny with our assignment. Heaven is my destiny, while bringing the Kingdom is my assignment. The focus of the Kingdom message is the rightful dominion of God over everything. Whatever is inconsistent with Heaven—namely, disease, torment, hatred, division, sin habits, etc.—must come under the authority of the King. These kinds of issues are broken off of people's lives because inferior realms cannot stand wherever the dominion of God becomes manifest. As we succeed in displaying this message, we are positioned to bring about cultural change in education, business, politics, the environment, and the other essential issues that we face today. This creates a most unusual phenomenon: the fruit of revival becomes the fuel of revival. And as long as we stay true to the message, the movement increases unto reformation.

QUESTIONS FOR REFLECTION

1. Explain the difference between the Gospel of salvation and the Gospel of the Kingdom. How is the Gospel of the Kingdom more holistic and all-encompassing, also including salvation?

_____

_____

_____

_____

_____

_____

2. How is the Gospel of the Kingdom both a message and a demonstration? What does the demonstration of the Kingdom look like, and what does seeing the Kingdom of God in action do for those witnessing these demonstrations?

_____

_____

_____

_____

_____

_____

_____

_____

_____

POINT OF REFLECTION: THE KINGDOM OF GOD IS IN THE SPIRIT OF GOD

The Kingdom of God is in the Holy Spirit, according to Romans 14:17. You are filled with the Spirit of God, and it is through His indwelling power that the Kingdom is released through you. Even Jesus, God incarnate, made Himself to be dependent upon the power of the Spirit to demonstrate the Kingdom through signs, wonders, miracles, and supernatural operation. By default, when the Spirit is released, the Kingdom comes onto the scene. When the Kingdom of God, which is the reign and rule of God, confronts sickness, oppression, torment, and all other expressions of the enemy, the Kingdom's superiority always overthrows the works of darkness.

The Message and the Harvest

*Since that time the kingdom of God has been
preached and everyone is pressing into it.*
—LUKE 16:16

Is it possible that the nature of the message determines the size of the harvest? Jesus did say *"everyone"!* While I do not believe in Universalism, where everyone eventually ends up in Heaven, the message of the Kingdom has a greater reach than I previously thought possible. This is the message: "His dominion is everlasting. It is *now.* Jesus' life demonstrated His dominion over everything that was inconsistent with God's will."

Don't skip over the bigger promises of Scripture simply because they are hard to believe because of their size. Whenever He declares something this big, He's hoping to capture people's hearts, making it impossible for them to be satisfied with mediocrity. Here He says, *"Everyone is pressing into it"* (Luke 16:16). In Joel 2:28, He says, *"I will pour out My Spirit on all flesh."* In Jeremiah 31:34, He states, *"All shall know Me."* Psalm 22, the psalm that deals with the crucifixion of Christ more than any other, states, *"All the ends of the world shall remember and turn to the Lord, and all the families of the nations shall worship before You"* (Ps. 22:27). This list of extraordinary promises could continue page after page. But you get the point. The promises are there, in a sense waiting for adoption. Instead of trying to figure out the season for the promises to be fulfilled, why not come before God and see if God might want to fulfill them in our time? After all, how many times did the disciples get the timing right in their understanding of God's prophetic promises? I don't consider myself any better than they were. These promises are not given to us to help us to know the future as much as they are given to create hunger for what might be. The promises of God are clearly seen when the people of God get hungry and cry out to God for their fulfillment. This is exactly what Daniel did in reading Jeremiah's prophecy. (See Daniel 9:2–6.) He turned the prophecies into prayers for his generation.

When you declare the right message, you create the atmosphere where everyone is able to press in. No matter the need, there is an answer now. The right message marries the truth of Jesus as the *desire of the nations* with the nations themselves. The right message changes the atmosphere to make the manifestation of His dominion realized. Perhaps this is the context in which the irresistible grace of God is embraced, thus fulfilling the desire found in the heart of every person alive.

QUESTIONS FOR REFLECTION

1. How might the nature of the message determine the size of the harvest (for example, the message of the Kingdom of God being both preached and demonstrated)?

_____

_____

_____

_____

_____

_____

_____

2. Explain what God's intention is for issuing a big promise. How does a big promise call you into a place of prayer and partnership with Him?

_____

_____

_____

_____

_____

_____

_____

_____

_____

PRAYER INVITATION

Lord, I receive Your invitation to agree with You in prayer.
I refuse to simply read over some of these major promises in Scripture and dismiss them.
I receive Your promises as a call to co-labor with You to see miraculous results.
Promises of all nations coming and worshiping You.
Promises of Your Spirit being poured out on all flesh.
Promises of Your name being feared because of Your goodness.
Promises of the Kingdom of God being preached and demonstrated…and everyone pressing into it!

The New Purpose of the Old Testament

For whatever was written in earlier times was written for
our instruction, so that through perseverance and the
encouragement of the Scriptures we might have hope.
—ROMANS 15:4 NASB

In this passage, Paul addresses the purpose for the study of the Old Testament. Please notice that correct study of Scripture is to give us *encouragement* that results in great *hope—that they might have hope.* And yet for many, the study of the Old Testament does anything but give them hope for their own lives. All many see are the judgments of God toward the nations. I believe if we get a different outcome than what this Romans passage said we would have (encouragement and hope), we must learn to approach the Scriptures differently until we bear His intended fruit.

The Old Testament was given for our instruction as New Covenant people. For a season the Old Testament Scriptures were the only Bible that the New Testament Church had. What has been written gives us the backdrop to the truths we enjoy today. But as it is with most things, improper application can also bring death. *"For the letter kills, but the Spirit gives life"* (2 Cor. 3:6). It's a matter of perception. Many Christians' lives have been crippled because of an unclear understanding of what Jesus came to accomplish and fulfill. If I don't understand that, I won't understand my purpose and calling. To put it more practically, through wisdom and revelation we must understand what of the Old Testament *ended at the cross*, what *was changed by the cross*, and what *came through the cross unchanged.*

QUESTIONS FOR REFLECTION

1. Read and reflect on Romans 15:4. Why is it so vital to have a correct perspective on the purpose of the Old Testament? What kind of wisdom and instruction does it offer for your everyday life?

_____

_____

_____

2. From your study of Scripture and reflection on the video session this week, explore the following:

    a. What ended at the cross:

    _____

    _____

    _____

    _____

    _____

    _____

    b. What changed at the cross:

    _____

    _____

    _____

    _____

    _____

    _____

    _____

    c. What came through the cross unchanged:

    _____

    _____

    _____

    _____

    _____

    _____

    _____

PRAYER

Holy Spirit, I ask You to show me the new purpose of the Old Covenant.
Help me to recognize what ended at the cross, what changed at the cross, and what came through the cross unchanged.
Thank You for the cross, Lord.
Thank You for that defining moment in history when everything changed.

God's Goodness Is Experienced in His Glorious Presence

*If the glory of God contains the revelation of
the goodness of God, then here is a key.
Jesus Christ dwelling in us by the Holy Spirit is
what makes the revelation of His goodness known
to and through us to the world around us.*

NOTES ON SESSION 4

" Understanding the nature of God invites us into a relationship with God.

❝ *Your faith will only explore the nature of God to the degree that you see Him as good.*

❝ *A coming revelation of the goodness of God upon the church will forever change our countenance.*

It's not correct to have the Old Testament with superior experience than what is offered in the New.

> **In the Kingdom of God, delayed answers are gaining interest.**

DISCUSSION QUESTIONS

1. Read Exodus 33:13 and Psalm 103:7. Why was Moses' request to know the ways of God so significant?

   a. What was the difference between Moses' encounter with the ways of God and Israel's experience with the acts of God?

2. How does your understanding of God's goodness determine how far you will go in your relationship with Him?

3. Explain the relationship between the glory of God and goodness of God.

4. Read Exodus 34:29–35. How does the goodness of God change our countenance?

   a. How will this help us accurately represent Jesus to the world around us?

5. Why do you think God wants worship? What happens to us in His Presence?

6. Read Second Chronicles 5:11–14. How is this account an invitation for you to encounter God's glory and Presence?

   a. What's different now that we are under the New Covenant?

7. Discuss what it looks like for God to inhabit praise (see Ps. 22:3).

8. Share some testimonies/stories of moments when you experienced the manifest Presence of God in times of worship.

   a. What impact did this time of worship have on the atmosphere around you?

   b. Share about different breakthroughs and miracles you experienced (or have witnessed) during worship?

ACTIVATION EXERCISE: ENCOUNTERING HIS GLORY AND GOODNESS

The goal of today's session was to explore the connection between the glory of God and the goodness of God. In the Old Testament, there are momentous encounters between different Bible characters and the Presence of God—notably, Moses in Exodus 33 and then the priests in Second Chronicles 5. When God's goodness is praised, God's glory manifests. When God's glory manifests on the scene, His Kingdom comes in power. It's not a formula; it's simply the great delight of every believer to live in the place that Jesus' blood restored them to *the glory*.

FAITH IN ACTION: ENCOURAGE WORSHIP

You will transition out of Group Discussion time and go right into a time of praise and worship. Whether you are using live worship leaders or recorded music, be sure that the focus is God's goodness and God's nature.

This week, spend time worshiping God following the model of Second Chronicles 5:11–14. The focus is God's good nature, as their song was *"the Lord is good."*

Here are some instructions:

- **Encourage *inconvenient* worship:** take a moment to minister to those who are currently going through circumstances or who are waiting on God for a certain answer, miracle, or breakthrough; encourage them to shift their focus from their need to the Lord. This is not pretending away the problem; it's simply elevating perspective to focus on the Solution.

- **Encourage *expectant* worship:** now that a vision has been presented of what we can expect in worship (under the Old Covenant), encourage participants to expect a visitation of God's Presence. Encourage them not to limit their expectation to one expression or manifestation (a cloud, flashing light, weight or heaviness, heat, etc.); simply encourage them to expect an encounter with God's goodness—whatever it looks like.

- **Encourage *extravagant* worship:** invite participants to engage with God in worship—clapping, lifting hands, shouting, dancing, etc. Whatever you would deem appropriate in the context (and as long as no one is distracting), encourage a fragrant and extravagant offering of worship to the Lord.

Day Sixteen

Your Invitation to Explore the Realms of God's Goodness

You will seek Me and...I will be found by you!
—Jeremiah 29:13-14

God invites us to discover Him, the One who rewards all who join in the journey into the great expanse called the goodness of God. This is the journey of faith, for faith believes *"that He is, and that He is a rewarder of those who diligently seek Him"* (Heb. 11:6).

Faith has two parts; the first is a conviction of His existence. But even the devil has that much going for him. It's the second part that launches us into the adventure and distinguishes us from the rest of all that exists—a confidence in His nature. He is a rewarder! In other words, what we believe about Him will have an effect on our lives in a measurable way because He rewards those who have set their hearts on discovering Him. He promises, *"You will seek Me and...I will be found by you!"* (Jer. 29:13–14). God ensures that we find Him if the heart is genuinely searching with a readiness to obey. Jesus also said He would disclose Himself to those who follow Him (see John 14:21). It's as though He is saying that if we seek Him with all of our hearts, He will make sure to put Himself in the middle of the road we're walking on.

This invitation comes from the Father of life—the eternal God who loves through sacrifice and giving. The greatest gift we could ever give ourselves is to anchor our intellect and will into the strongest foundation possible—the goodness of God.

QUESTIONS FOR REFLECTION

1. Based on the Scripture passages you read today, how is God inviting you to seek Him out?

_____

_____

_____

_____

_____
_____
_____
_____
_____
_____
_____

2.   What is the key to actually finding God? (Clue: there is a posture your heart needs to maintain in order to discover and experience Him.)

_____
_____
_____
_____
_____
_____
_____
_____
_____
_____
_____
_____

PRAYER OF INVITATION

Lord, I receive Your invitation.
I seek You with the expectation of finding You.
You invite me into a place of discovering Your goodness and experiencing Your Presence.
This means I should set out on this journey expecting to meet You.
Holy Spirit, may I be ready and willing to obey as I seek You.
May I be ready and willing to follow You.
I say "Yes," God.
I say "Yes" to this quest of discovering You.
But I also say "Yes" to whatever You ask of me.

CULTIVATING THE HEART OF AN EXPLORER

Call to me and I will answer you. I'll tell you marvelous and
wondrous things that you could never figure out on your own.
—JEREMIAH 33:3 MSG

We are all explorers, searching for the new, enjoying the old, becoming personally enlarged with each discovery. What we behold affects us. If we look at it long enough, it changes us. There are parts of God's goodness that are easily noticeable to the casual observer. Much like Moses, we've been given a challenge. He saw a burning bush that wasn't being consumed by its flames. The story records an important detail that should help us all in our journey. It was only when Moses turned aside that the Lord spoke to him from the bush. (See Exodus 3:4.) Sometimes giving undivided attention to the obvious releases a greater encounter with Him, manifesting a greater revelation of what He is like. The bottom line is that we can't find anything significant on our own. It must be revealed to us. In other words, all discoveries are not the result of our discipline and determination alone. As the ultimate steward, He gives these gifts to those who have embraced His invitation to ask, seek, and knock.

The prophet Jeremiah caught a glimpse of this reality when God gave him a promise of restoration. *"Call to Me and I will answer you, and I will tell you great and mighty things, which you do not know"* (Jer. 33:3 NASB). The God who is good gave us the invitation to call upon Him. He then promised to answer in a way that was beyond what we asked for. The word *great* in this verse means "considerably above average." And if that weren't enough, He follows the word *great* with the word *mighty*. *Mighty* means "inaccessible." Consider this: God has given us access to the inaccessible. What an incomprehensible promise! It is out of the reach of our skills, character, or qualifications. We lack all that is necessary to be able to apprehend what exists in the realm called the goodness of God. But He gave us something that makes this impossibility possible. He gave us the key to the inaccessible. He Himself is that key. Through His name we have access to that which is beyond our reach on our best day. The invitation came from His goodness. He invites us to call upon Him, giving Him the open door to answer in a way that is above our expectations and imagination. There is no goodness apart from Him, so our journey is a discovery of the person of God—the One whose inaccessible goodness is now accessible by an invitation with His promise *to be found by us*.

QUESTIONS FOR REFLECTION

1. Explain why "beholding" God's goodness can transform you. Identify some practical ways that you can "behold" God's goodness in your everyday life.

    _____

    _____

    _____

    _____

    _____

2. Describe how an invitation like Jeremiah 33:3 should cultivate a lifestyle of hunger in your life for God? Explain how meditating on this invitation and living mindful of its possibilities should be able to fuel your lifelong pursuit of God.

    _____

    _____

    _____

    _____

    _____

    _____

    _____

PRAYER OF PURSUIT

Lord, You have invited me to pursue You.
Even though You live inside of me, in full, I am experiencing You in part.
I see in part, taste in part, encounter in part.
This doesn't discourage me; it fuels my hunger to experience more of You.
Father, I ask You to come right now and overwhelm me with the revelation of Your goodness.
Your greatness is unsearchable.
Your goodness is beyond comprehension.
Help me to live mindful of these truths.
Even though Your goodness is beyond my comprehension, it is not beyond my experience.
I will experience in part while living on earth, but every experience gives me a greater glimpse.
Every experience in Your Presence gives me a richer taste.
Every experience satisfies the deepest parts of my heart and also leaves me hungry for more.
Thank You, God, for the gift of hunger!
It's this gift that draws me into unexplored realms of Your Presence and goodness.

Exploring His Glory

And he said, "Please, show me Your glory." Then He said, "I will make all My
goodness pass before you, and I will proclaim the name of the Lord before you."
—EXODUS 33:18-19

When Moses asked to see the glory of God, he did not choose some random aspect of God's person or nature. He chose the original target for every person alive. We were created and designed to live in the glory of God, which is the manifested Presence of Jesus. The Scripture says, *"For all have sinned and fall short of the glory of God"* (Rom. 3:23). Sin caused us to fall short of God's intended target. *To sin* means "to miss the mark." Consider an archer shooting an arrow at a target and then watching that arrow not even reach the target, let alone hit the bull's-eye. That is what our sin has done. We not only missed the mark; we didn't even reach the target. But take note of the target—it is the glory of God. We were created to live in that realm. Moses knew it instinctively and longed to see it more clearly.

Consider all the encounters that Moses had with God. The glory of God was present in the burning bush, during the many times on the mountain where God descended upon Moses and spoke, and through the visitations in the tent of meeting, which was also filled with His glory. These are just a few of the examples listed in Scripture. Yet in this moment there was only one thing in his mind—the glory. All of those encounters had an effect on Moses, and then upon Israel. Once you've tasted of the real reason that you're alive, nothing else will ever satisfy. But this particular encounter with God in His glory is the only time Moses' face shone like God's. I think it's important to notice what was unique about this encounter. It's the only time people feared the appearance of Moses, and they had him put a cloth over his head to protect them from what they were seeing upon him. I have this deep personal sense that the glory of God will be a primary subject and passion of the Church in the coming years.

QUESTIONS FOR REFLECTION

1. Reflect and meditate on Romans 3:23. How does this passage of Scripture extend an invitation to you to live in the glory of God?

_____
_____
_____
_____
_____
_____
_____
_____
_____
_____
_____

2.   Explain how experiencing the glory of God satisfies you at the deepest level imaginable?

_____
_____
_____
_____
_____
_____
_____
_____
_____
_____
_____

MEDITATION: SECOND CORINTHIANS 3

Now that you are halfway through the week's readings, it is important that you reconsider the fact that, because of Jesus, you are living under the New Covenant. This is a new and *better* Covenant, according to Hebrews 7:22 and 8:6. If this Covenant contains *better* promises, it is important for you to read Paul's powerful description of your New Covenant access to God's glory. Read Second Corinthians 3 and reflect on what God has made available to you that's even greater than what Moses and the priests in the Old Testament enjoyed. This is designed to help take your hunger for God to new levels, as it's hunger that escorts you into experience.

HIS DWELLING PLACE

Don't you realize that all of you together are the temple
of God and that the Spirit of God lives in you?
—1 CORINTHIANS 3:16 NLT

I remember a number of years ago we had a prophetic song during one of our Sunday morning services. We call this type of song "the song of the Lord" in that it is a prophetic song, sung as though it were His voice singing over us as His people. It went something like this:

> *Did I not fill the tabernacle of Moses with My glory?*
> *Did I not fill the temple of Solomon with My glory?*
> *How much more should I fill the place that I build with My own hands?*
> *My beloved, I am building you.*

In that moment we realized that God was referring to the Matthew 16:18 passage where Jesus said, *"I will build My church."* So here it is, a chance to catch a glimpse of where God puts His glory and why. He was not ashamed to put His glory upon and in the physical buildings that people built in honor of His name. How much more will He put the glory in the house that He Himself builds? And that house is the *Church*—the eternal dwelling place of God. (See Ephesians 2:22.)

Obviously, I make no references to institutions or buildings when I say "Church." Those elements are good and useful tools of the actual Church. But they in themselves are not the Church. The Church is comprised of born-again believers who are as living stones, brought together into a spiritual house, to house a priesthood that will offer spiritual sacrifices, acceptable through Jesus. That is the revelation that Peter carried for us. (See First Peter 2:5.)

And to take it one step further, the glory that is put within that house is to manifest the goodness of God, or we miss the point altogether.

QUESTIONS FOR REFLECTION

1. Explain how the church has now been designated to be the dwelling place of God. How did protocol transition from the Old to New Testament when it came to where God's glory would dwell?

    _____

    _____

    _____

    _____

    _____

    _____

    _____

    _____

    _____

    _____

    _____

    _____

    _____

    _____

    _____

    _____

    _____

    _____

    _____

    _____

    _____

2. The Holy Spirit already lives inside of you. What do you think are the keys to seeing more of the Spirit's Presence released on and through your life?

    _____

    _____

    _____

    _____

PRAYER OF ACTIVATION

Father, You said that I am Your dwelling place.

Jesus paid a high price so that Your Presence did not have to remain in a tent or temple.

I thank You, God, for the great work the church is accomplishing across the earth.

Thank You, Lord, for the masses who are coming to Christ, being discipled, and trained to represent You.

I bless and celebrate Your work.

I honor Your leaders.

But God, right now, I ask for more. And it starts with me.

Lord, You've made Your indwelling glory available to me.

Holy Spirit, You already live on the inside me.

You're here, now.

I ask for You to show me how to cooperate with You in a greater way.

Show me how to yield every area of my life, my thinking, and my attitudes to Your influence.

I am forever grateful You've come to dwell within me; now, I ask for the more.

I ask for You to rest upon my life in power.

More, Lord!

And as I ask You for more of Your Presence and power, help me to give You more of me.

Day Twenty

CHRIST IN YOU: THE HOPE OF GLORY

Christ in you, the hope of glory.
—COLOSSIANS 1:27

The focus of the prophets, as well as the prophetic experiences contained throughout the Scriptures, oftentimes points to God's purposes for His people, the Church. The stories referenced in this study reveal God's heart and plans for us. He has purposed to manifest Himself upon us and through us and, as a result, to transform the nature of the world around us. This must be seen, embraced, and received as a part of our *reason for being*.

The target of the Lord for us is still the glory. His glory is to become the dwelling place of God's people, as He in turn dwells in us. The apostle Paul used a phrase that is to grab our hearts: *"Christ in you, the hope of glory"* (Col. 1:27). Jesus Christ in us makes it possible to be restored fully to His purpose for us—living in the glory.

If the glory of God contains the revelation of the goodness of God, then here is a key. Jesus Christ dwelling in us by the Holy Spirit is what makes the revelation of His goodness known to and through us to the world around us. And that is hope illustrated.

QUESTIONS FOR REFLECTION

1. Based on your daily reading, what would you conclude are some of the objectives of God's glory dwelling in and upon you?

_____

_____

_____

_____

_____

_____

_____
_____
_____
_____
_____
_____
_____
_____

2. Reflect and meditate on Colossians 1:27. Explore what that statement means: Christ in you, the hope of glory.

_____
_____
_____
_____
_____
_____
_____
_____
_____
_____
_____
_____
_____

PRAYER OF REVELATION

Father, I ask You to open my eyes to have a clearer vision of "Christ in me, the hope of glory."
Thank You that I carry Your glory.
Thank You for the price You paid for the Holy Spirit to live in me.
I praise You for this glorious gift.
May the world and environment around me see Jesus in a clearer way through my life as I represent Your goodness.

GOD'S GOODNESS EXPRESSED THROUGH PERFECT JUDGMENT

We are the most useless in our faith when our confidence for transformation depends on the return of Christ instead of the work of Christ. His return will be glorious! But His work sets the stage for a transformed people to transform the nature of the world they live in.

NOTES ON SESSION 5

> *Jesus took the judgment that mankind deserved so we could step into the freedom He deserved.*

" *Blessing on an unsanctified life crushes it; blessing on a sanctified life establishes it.*

" *A massive revival to the nations could come because of the blessing of God on His people.*

> *Gifts are free; maturity is expensive.*

> **When God brings discipline, it's always from His love and compassion.**

DISCUSSION QUESTIONS

1. Read Psalm 27:13. How is the truth of God's goodness your anchor and keep you from losing heart?

    a. How does God's goodness actually keep your heart safe from the problems and turmoil around you?

2. What is the difference between God approving tragedy and God causing tragedy? (Is there a difference?)

3. Why should we actually love judgment?

    a. What is God's judgment actually aimed at?

4. Explore this question: Why doesn't God get rid of all evil and sin in a single moment of time? How does this reveal His love, justice, and goodness?

5. Why do you think we need to change our perspective when it comes to the last days?

    a. Specifically, how do we need to change our view of the last days conditions presented in Matthew 24?

    b. How are end-times conditions not promises of God? How should we respond to the conditions that Jesus is describing?

6. How did Pastor Bill's message give you an encouraging perspective on the last days? Discuss how your concept of the last days actually shapes your everyday life.

7. Read Jeremiah 33:9 and Hosea 3:5. Explain how God's goodness can release the "fear" or trembling of the Lord. What do you think this looks like on your life?

8. How does God discipline His people through the word He speaks to them? What is the end result of His judgment?

9. Read Psalm 67. How does God's blessing and goodness demonstrated upon your life have the ability to impact nations?

    a. Share testimony of how God's blessing on your life has actually invited others to know God.

ACTIVATION EXERCISE: HIS JUDGMENT CALLS YOU INTO MATURITY AND DEVELOPMENT

The goal of today's session was to have an accurate, New Covenant perspective on the judgment of God. It reveals His holiness and also is a key method for maturing His people. It's important, however, for the believer not to fear judgment but embrace it. God disciplines not to put you down, but to call you higher. He speaks His cleansing word to you, just as Jesus spoke His word to the disciples, and calls you into new places of maturity so you can be a fit carrier of the manifest goodness of God.

Judgment begins in the house of the Lord for a reason—if it started in the world, it would be condemnation, because those without Christ would be judged as lost. It begins among the community of God's people not to condemn or punish, but to invite you to be a fit vessel to carry a measure of God's blessing that is so outstanding that the on-looking world sees it and takes notice.

FAITH IN ACTION: RELEASING HIS GOODNESS

The end goal of God's discipline and judgment in your life—*to be a carrier of His goodness*. His objective is that in these last days, the people around you would see the evidence of God's goodness in your life and respond with *fear*. Trembling. Awe.

This all begins with the invitation of Psalm 67:1-2:

> *God be merciful to us and bless us,*
> *And cause His face to shine upon us, Selah*
> *That Your way may be known on earth,*
> *Your salvation among all nations.*

Take this time to pray this prayer over the participants. You can have different group members pray or break up into smaller groups/prayer partners. Here are some prayer directives to get you started.

- Pray for God's blessing to overwhelm every person and be visible on their lives.

- Pray for God's blessing to be demonstrated on households, businesses, and communities.

- Pray that each person would respond to the invitation of God's discipline and recognize how He disciplines His people today.

- Pray for an outpouring of God's goodness on His people so that nations would be drawn to Jesus and find salvation.

- Pray for the right perspective on the last days; ask the Holy Spirit to empower each person to be a transformational ambassador who is not put off by the conditions of the world but who responds faithfully to the commission of Jesus.

Why We Should Love Judgment

All of God's judgments are aimed at whatever interferes with love.
—Mike Bickle

If you take someone you love to the doctor to be examined because of a suspicious-looking growth on his arm, you will want that doctor to bring judgment upon the growth and do whatever needs to be done to remove it. You'll not pick a doctor that shows mercy to the growth or one who becomes fascinated with how it is its own living entity. Only judgment is acceptable. I realize that sounds pretty silly at best to have a doctor who thinks like that, but I say it to make a point. There's no feeling of sympathy toward the tumor, neither is there any concern over what others might think. Judgment is the only acceptable response, as your love for that person requires such a reaction toward anything that threatens his well-being. Love requires that I fight for him by seeking for his protection. We live in a world where we celebrate judgments all the time. But for some reason, if the judgment comes from God, it's considered cruel and unloving. My friend Mike Bickle made a statement on this subject that really helped bring clarification for me in this issue: "All of God's judgments are aimed at whatever interferes with love." Priceless. And so completely true.

If I had a neighbor that showed aggression and violence toward children, I would do whatever I could to inform the authorities and protect the children. While I tend to lean toward mercy for people who are caught up in sin, I would refuse to do anything that would protect their sinfulness, which would continue to threaten the safety of others. Such carelessness toward "friends" is not love at all. Love stands for something. It is honest and confrontational when necessary. For example, it is not love to see someone you care for in a burning building and leave her there, no matter how sincere she is, or how good of a person she is, or how rough her childhood was. Love requires action. Love requires judgment—"This building is on fire. Get out or you will die!"

Love chooses the best. Love doesn't choose what simply feels good to us.

QUESTIONS FOR REFLECTION

1. How do you understand the quote from Mike Bickle? How are God's judgments aimed at what interferes with His love?

    _____

    _____

    _____

    _____

    _____

    _____

    _____

    _____

    _____

    _____

2. Why should you actually love God's judgment? (Refer to the illustration of the doctor hating the cancerous growth.)

    _____

    _____

    _____

    _____

    _____

    _____

    _____

    _____

    _____

POINT OF MEDITATION

The judgment of God is a controversial subject. Nevertheless, it is scriptural and it must be studied. The challenging portions in the Bible should never turn us away but should invite us into a conversation with the Holy Spirit. In the upcoming daily readings and reflections, ask the Holy Spirit to lead you through the process of understanding God's judgment as an expression of His goodness.

CONDEMNATION IS NOT GOD'S HEART

*Do I have any pleasure at all that the wicked should die...
and not that he should turn from his ways and live?*
—EZEKIEL 18:23

Let's take the subject of God's judgment a step further. First, let's recognize that if God were hell-bent on bringing condemnation on all mankind, He could and would have accomplished that a long time ago by simply declaring the word needed to bring it about. The whole point of this teaching is that condemnation is not in His heart. We clearly see in Scripture that God takes no pleasure in the death of the wicked (see Ezek. 18:23). Yet the fact remains, judgment has to happen because God is holy—He is perfect in beauty, with undefiled purity, completely separate from all that is dark and evil and totally driven by love in all actions, thoughts, and intentions. Sin violates and contaminates all that He has made, creating a breach between Creator and creation. Yet judgment had to be released because He is love. Out of necessity He declared, *"The soul who sins shall die"* (Ezek. 18:20). That was something that came forth because He is love. Please notice that statement is in the same chapter as *"Do I have any pleasure at all that the wicked should die...and not that he should turn from his ways and live?"* (Ezek. 18:23).

God cannot lie—it would be an impossible violation of His nature and being. But the most amazing thing happened. God chose to pour out the much-needed judgment upon His Son, Jesus, instead of us. Because of His great love for us, Jesus volunteered to take our place in bearing the penalty of death that each of us deserved. In doing so, He satisfied the appetite of the Law for our judgment. And if that weren't enough, He then qualified us to receive the inheritance that only Jesus deserved. I remind you that He alone is the One who lived without sin, blemish, or compromise of any kind. In all honesty, I would have been totally satisfied to have my appointment with hell cancelled. But for the Father to qualify me for the same reward as Jesus? That is as far beyond my grasp as any thought or idea could possibly be.

QUESTIONS FOR REFLECTION

1. Reflect on Ezekiel 18:23 and Second Peter 3:9. How do passages like these reveal God's heart that none should be condemned?

_____

_____

_____

_____

_____

_____

_____

_____

_____

_____

_____

_____

_____

_____

_____

_____

_____

_____

_____

_____

2. How does the redemptive work of Jesus fulfill the righteous requirments of God's judgment?

_____

_____

_____

DECLARATION OF PRAISE

Thank You, Jesus, for taking the punishment and judgment that I deserved.
I am covered by Your blood.
You call me Your son/daughter.
You have adopted me into Your family and translated me out of darkness.
I praise You for this!

PRAYER OF REFLECTION

Lord, help me to always live mindful of what You have delivered me from.
May this fuel my compassion toward others, knowing that Your will is to save them.
Deliver them.
Restore them.
Show Yourself good to them.
May I represent You like this to the world around me.

Day Twenty-Three

A New Perspective on the Last Days

There are many promises concerning the last days. Truth be told, we have been living in the last days for two thousand years. The prophet Joel spoke of the outpouring of the Holy Spirit in Acts 2 as that which would take place *"in the last days"* (Acts 2:17). So if those were the last days, we are certainly in the last of the last days.

Jesus had much to say about the days we live in. For example, He said we would be hearing of *"wars and rumors of wars…for nation will rise up against nation…and in various places there will be famines and earthquakes"* (Matt. 24:6-7 NASB). It's important to note that Jesus wasn't giving His people a promise. In other words, this was not a word that the Church was to exercise their faith over to bring about what God had purposed. Instead, Jesus is simply describing the conditions into which He was sending His last days' army with transformational influence.

Everyone's *last days' theology* requires faith. For some it is a faith to endure until we're rescued. For others it's a faith to obtain in response to our commission. I'll take the latter. We are the most useless in our faith when our confidence for transformation depends on the return of Christ instead of the work of Christ. His return will be glorious! But His redemptive work set the stage for a transformed people to transform the nature of the world they live in. It is a glorious work, being done by a glorious bride that the Glorious One will return for.

QUESTIONS FOR REFLECTION

1. Regardless of what you believe about the end times, why do you think it's important to focus on Jesus' transformational strategy for the world instead of just escaping to Heaven (and history wrapping up)?

_____
_____
_____
_____
_____
_____
_____

2.   Explain how your personal theology of the last days requires faith.

_____
_____
_____
_____
_____
_____
_____
_____
_____
_____
_____

PRAYER OF INFLUENCE FOR HIS GOODNESS

Father, raise up Kingdom influencers in these last days—those who are an influence for good with the message of Your goodness.

Wherever I am, right now, I choose to be an influencer for Your goodness.

I'm not waiting to get to my "next level" or "big break."

I choose to be a Kingdom influencer, right here and right now.

I ask You, Lord, to cause Your Spirit to rest upon me.

Rest upon my words.

Rest upon my interactions with people.

Rest upon my attitudes, when people are watching and when they are not.

Rest upon me so that Your goodness would be a visible reality in my life.

END-TIME PROMISES THAT YOU CAN CLAIM

When God gives us a promise, it's as though He has gone into our future and brought back the word needed to get us to where He wants us to be. And so it is with these two brilliant promises of God for His people of the last days.

> *Afterward the children of Israel shall return and seek the Lord their God and David their king. They shall fear the Lord and His goodness in the latter days* (Hosea 3:5).

Notice that there is a connection between seeking God, God's goodness, and people fearing Him, with the last days as the setting for the fulfillment of this promise. I suggest we use our faith to believe for what was promised here.

> *Then it shall be to Me a name of joy, a praise, and an honor before all nations of the earth, who shall hear all the good that I do to them; they shall fear and tremble for all the goodness and all the prosperity that I provide for it* (Jeremiah 33:9).

These are two startling promises given by God. I don't remember ever hearing a preacher who specialized in the last days talking about these passages, nor even the subjects they address. The promise is clear—God's goodness will be seen upon His people. Consider this: it just might be that the most overlooked evangelistic tool of the Church is the blessing of the Lord upon our lives. We've seen blessings abused, materialistic kingdoms built in His name, and other self-centered expressions. But when we react to the errors of others, we are prone to create yet another error.

The Bible says that others will see His goodness and will in turn fear the Lord. I wonder, how good does that goodness have to be for people to see it and actually tremble? It's hard to imagine His goodness in a casual or incidental manner bringing about that response. It would have to be so clear, and in my opinion so *extreme*, so as to be obviously manifested from God Himself, that people tremble with fear.

Put on your seat belts! We're about to enter the journey of a lifetime. It's a time where opposition increases, the need for our help becomes more obvious, and the blessing of God separates us from others. Knowing how to steward such things is paramount to our fulfilling His heart to disciple nations.

QUESTIONS FOR REFLECTION

1. Meditate on the two promises that were presented in your daily reading: Hosea 3:5 and Jeremiah 33:9. Ask the Holy Spirit to speak to you about what's being communicated in these passages and write down your thoughts in the lined space below.

_____

_____

_____

_____

_____

_____

_____

_____

_____

_____

_____

_____

_____

_____

_____

_____

_____

2. Explain how you think the goodness of God will cause people to tremble. What do you think His goodness has to look like upon your life in order for this to happen?

_____

_____

MEDITATION FOR TRANSFORMATION

Continue to reflect on the two passages from Scripture that were in your daily reading. Ask the Lord to lead you to other promises, like these, that give you a vision of what to pray into in these last days. Even though God is the righteous judge and He promises to execute justice, these other promises are just as valid and accurately represent His heart of goodness. He desires that all people would see His goodness, tremble, and respond to the invitation. He wants you to show how the God who is good to you desires to be good to others. Remember, though, He wants to not only tell this through words, but He wants to show it.

CALLING THE WORLD TO ENCOUNTER HIS GOODNESS

God be merciful to us and bless us, and cause His face to shine upon us, Selah,
that Your way may be known on earth, Your salvation among all nations.
—PSALM 67:1-2

Blessings are manifestations of increased favor. Yet favor has a purpose. Without discovering that purpose, we are prone to self-promotion and personal kingdom building. The queen of Sheba put it this way when she acknowledged the favor that rested upon Solomon: *"Blessed be the Lord your God who delighted in you to set you on the throne of Israel; because the Lord loved Israel forever, therefore He made you king, to do justice and righteousness"* (1 Kings 10:9). There it is. Because God loved Israel, He showed favor upon Solomon and made him king. Favor was to benefit those he served as king or it would be misused. It basically comes down to this: *favor upon me must benefit the people under my influence, or it is misused.*

We are coming into increased times of favor and blessing, with greater and greater areas of responsibility. I'm not saying we're coming into a life of ease and self-exalting bounty. It's just that He is making it more and more obvious who carries His heart by releasing an increased favor upon them for influence. That is that mark of His blessing.

Our positions of increase are unto something. The problems that our cities and nations are facing have no answers outside of God. We, the people of unfailing hope, have the opportunity to serve and serve well, bringing the King and His Kingdom into the everyday lives of people all around us. He is putting something upon us that will help them to see Him. If I use that which God is placing into my charge for personal gain, I will find myself seriously disappointed. But if I can live with His favor and blessing and use it for its intended purpose, nations will turn to Christ. That is His promise. That is His Word. And it is so, because He is good.

QUESTIONS FOR REFLECTION

1. Consider Psalm 67—the prayer of blessing and the end result of nations experiencing salvation. Even though there is a day of future judgment coming, explain how God wants to bless you in order for the world around you to get a picture of what God is like and receive salvation.

2. Explain how your blessing, increase, and influence can reveal a good Father to a world that doesn't know what God looks like.

_____

3. What does it look like to be a "good steward" of God's blessing and favor?

_____

PRAYER OF BLESSING

Use Psalm 67 as a template for your prayer:

> *God be merciful to us and bless us,*
> *And cause His face to shine upon us, Selah*
> *That Your way may be known on earth,*
> *Your salvation among all nations* (Psalm 67:1-2).

> *God, Your desire is for Your way to be known on the earth, and nations to receive the salvation found in Jesus.*
> *Show me how to show Your way to the world around me.*
> *To my family, my school, my workplace, my business.*
> *May Your way be known in and through my life and may those around me experience Your transforming life!*

God's Goodness Displayed in Jesus Christ: Perfect Theology

Whatever you think you know about God that you can't find in the person of Jesus you have reason to question. Jesus Christ is the fullest and most precise revelation of the Father and His nature that could ever be made known.

NOTES ON SESSION 6

**Jesus Christ is perfect theology.**

❝ *Anything that you think you know about God that you can't find in the person of Jesus, you have reason to question.* ❞

> **If we misjudge who the Father is, we will misrepresent Him.**

DISCUSSION QUESTIONS

1. Discuss the statement, "Jesus Christ is perfect theology."

2. Based on Pastor's Bill teaching, what was the primary reason that Jesus came to earth?

3. **Review John 10:10.** How can you identify the "fingerprints of the enemy"?

   a. How does this passage help differentiate between what comes from God and the devil?

4. What did Jesus come to reveal about the Father? Discuss as a group.

   a. How did God give us a picture of how He responds to problems?

5. Discuss this statement: "If we misjudge who the Father is, we will misrepresent Him." Why is it so important that we know what the Father is like when it comes to representing Him?

6. How does Jesus' interaction with the following two individuals reveal God the Father? What do they say about who God is?

   a. Blind Bartimaeus (see Mark 10:46–52)

   b. Woman caught in the act of adultery (see John 8:1–11)

7. Discuss how Jesus performed His works and miracles because He was anointed by the Holy Spirit. What does this mean to us and how do we respond?

8. What are the two conditions needed to model Jesus and operate in His supernatural power?

9. What should we do when we do not receive breakthrough and answered prayer? What did the disciples do and how should we follow their example?

ACTIVATION EXERCISE: FOLLOWING JESUS' EXAMPLE

The goal of today's session was to clearly reveal that Jesus came to show us what God the Father is like. Everything Jesus did is an expression of God's nature and character. He only did what He saw the Father do and said what He heard the Father speak.

The unchanging identity of Jesus as perfect theology is a constant invitation for you to keep praying, believing, and persevering for breakthrough. If Jesus is the ultimate revelation of God's character and will, then Jesus' works give us a very clear blueprint of what God would *want* done.

Today, we are going to ask the Holy Spirit to come and stir us to believe for breakthrough again—not because of what we've seen or haven't seen, but on the basis of who God is and what He revealed about Himself through the person of Jesus Christ.

FAITH IN ACTION: HOW EMPOWERED BY THE HOLY SPIRIT ARE YOU WILLING TO BE?

Jesus set an example that could be followed; the question is—how empowered by the Holy Spirit are you willing to be?

Because of Jesus' blood, you are completely and utterly cleansed of sin. You are totally forgiven and thus qualified to be filled with the Spirit and move in God's miracle-working power.

Unfortunately, due to disappointment or lack of results, many have retreated from their call to represent Jesus through the demonstration of healing, power, and miracles.

The reality of unanswered prayers in our lives doesn't change the facts about God that Jesus clearly displayed. We don't try to pretend these situations or losses away; rather, we continue to keep Jesus as the standard and *ask Him for a greater measure of anointing to be released through our lives.*

- Get alone with God and cry out.

- Go into public and take risks.

Take this time of prayer and activation to cry out to God once again.

- Pray God's promises of healing and deliverance, declaring that they are His will.

- Ask for a greater measure of empowerment by the Holy Spirit.

- Pray for those who have experienced loss and disappointment—that the Spirit of God would bring them unusual comfort and refreshing.

- Ask for the goodness of Jesus to be clearly displayed through the people.

- Ask for opportunities this week to get out in public and take risks.

- Ask for boldness and empowerment to pray for those God highlights.

- Ask for supernatural discernment and sensitivity to the Spirit's leading.

Day Twenty-Six

JESUS CAME TO REVEAL A GOOD FATHER

The Son is the dazzling radiance of God's splendor, the exact
expression of God's true nature—His mirror image!
—HEBREWS 1:3 TPT

Both the mystery and the revelation of God's goodness are contained in Jesus. In reading through the Gospel of John, the gospel that contains the bulk of the revelation of why Jesus came to earth, we find out that when we see Jesus, we see the Father. (See John 14:9.) We then discover that He says only what the Father is saying. (See John 12:49–50.) We also come to realize that Jesus does only what the Father is doing. (See John 5:19.) And so everything that we love and admire about Jesus is actually a precise and calculated manifestation of the Father. God is *the* Father, and the Father is good.

Hebrews 1:1-3 is a stunning section of Scripture. It tells us that Jesus is the exact representation of the Father—His nature and His person. He is that which emanates from the Father's being, manifesting His glory (remember goodness, Exodus 33:18–19). It's interesting to note that when Jesus informed the disciples that He was going back to the Father, but that He would send the Comforter (the Holy Spirit), He used a very specific word. *"I will ask the Father, and He will give you another Helper, that He may be with you forever"* (John 14:16 NASB). The word used here for "another" means *one that is exactly the same*. Let me illustrate. As I write this book, I'm looking at the furniture in my living room. There are two couches facing each other in front of a fireplace. They are exactly the same—mirror images of each other. We have another couch in our family room, but its color, shape, and size are quite a bit different from the two in our living room. I could accurately say, "I have *another* couch in my family room." But I couldn't use the word used in John 14, because, while my family room couch qualifies as a couch, it isn't exactly the same as the two in my living room. What's the point? When we look at Jesus, He is *exactly* the same as His Father. Then Jesus sent the Holy Spirit, who is *exactly* like Jesus. In other words, God wanted to make sure that there would be no chance of missing the revelation needed to permeate and shift the course of history at this point and time—the revelation of our God as a good and perfect Father.

Jesus reveals a Father who is not abusive or self-serving. The Holy Spirit, who now lives in us, reaffirms the wonder and beauty of this perfectly good Father. The work that He is doing in us is all about deepening our connection to the Father, who brings identity, purpose, destiny, and an awareness

GOD IS GOOD INTERACTIVE MANUAL

of unlimited resources to accomplish our purpose in life. When the Holy Spirit is able to do His perfect work in us, our connection to all that is good is strengthened and made clear. This revelation of God as our Father is the ultimate expression of the goodness of God.

QUESTIONS FOR REFLECTION

1. Explain how the person of Jesus Christ should be your final authority in revealing what God the Father is like.

_____

_____

_____

_____

_____

_____

_____

2. Why is it so important that you understand the truth, "The Son is exactly like the Father"? How does this give you clarity on recognizing what forces are beyond what's going on in your life and how to boldly respond to circumstances that come against you?

_____

_____

_____

_____

_____

_____

_____

POINT OF REFLECTION

Jesus Christ, the Son of God, is the exact representation and expression of God the Father. There is no generation loss between the two. Everything that Jesus reveals through His words and actions clearly demonstrates what God the Father would say and what He would do.

Jesus Reveals the Father to Blind Bartimaeus and a Woman Caught in Adultery

Jesus replied...anyone who has seen me has seen the Father!
—John 14:9 NLT

Everything Jesus said and did worked to fulfill that one assignment—reveal the Father. When I realized that simple point, it changed everything. It created a context and, more importantly, a reason for every word and action of Jesus. The Father was to be made known to this planet of orphans.

When Jesus responded to the cry of blind Bartimaeus, He was representing the Father. There's not one of us, if we had the ability to turn our blind child into a seeing child, that wouldn't do it. It's what fathers do. We fix things. And in this case, Jesus took care of his blindness by opening his eyes, but he also gave him a new identity. The blind man threw aside his beggar's garment when he came to Jesus. That garment was his badge of employment, given by the priests, to prove he was deserving of alms.

When they brought the woman caught in adultery to Jesus to see what He would do, He once again represented the Father. The religious leaders brought stones to kill her according to the Law they lived under. But Jesus came with a different assignment. He bent over and wrote in the dirt, telling those intending to stone her to go ahead, under this condition: the one without sin cast the first stone (see John 8:7). Interestingly, the only one without sin refused to cast a stone at all. Instead, He revealed the Father. In reality, this was a Father/daughter moment.

All those intending to stone her to death fled the scene. Whatever He wrote released such an atmosphere of grace that those driven by judgment had to leave. Jesus then did what any one of us would have done if our daughter were lost in such moral failure and humiliating shame. He served her. Jesus didn't care what the religious leaders thought of Him. The opinions of the crowd didn't matter either. The Father had to be seen. And more importantly, the Father had to be known by this one who was lost, this one who was manifesting her orphaned heart.

QUESTIONS FOR REFLECTION

1. Review the interaction that Jesus had with Blind Bartimaeus (Mark 10:46–52). What does Jesus' response to this man reveal about God the Father?

_____

_____

_____

_____

_____

_____

_____

_____

_____

2. Review the interaction that Jesus had with the woman caught in the act of adultery (John 8:1–11). What does Jesus' response to this man reveal about God the Father?

_____

_____

_____

_____

_____

_____

_____

_____

POINT OF REFLECTION

Study Jesus' interactions throughout the Gospels. Every interaction that someone had with Jesus was an encounter with God the Father. Every exchange with Jesus is significant, with no word or action happening by chance. Each one invites you to behold and know the Father in a deeper way. Ask the Lord for a new perspective when reading through the Gospels—that you would see the Father through the works and words of Jesus, the Son.

JESUS REVIEWS HIS ASSIGNMENT

*And this is eternal life, that they may know You, the only
true God, and Jesus Christ whom You have sent.*
—JOHN 17:3

The priestly prayer of Jesus in John 17 opens for us some of the most intimate moments between Jesus and His Father. To me it sounds like Jesus is giving an account of how He spent His time on planet Earth to His Father. The entire chapter is worth reading just for this single purpose—how did Jesus give an account of His life on earth? Just seeing this helps us to see the understanding that Jesus had in what He was to do in coming to this planet. Jesus mentions many things in His prayer, but there are four things I'd like to list from this great chapter:

1. Jesus came to finish the work of the Father. Remember, it's the family business that Jesus continued in, touching and healing people's lives. *"If I do not do the works of My Father, do not believe Me"* (John 10:37). Encountering the work of the Father introduces that person to the Father Himself. *"Believe the works, that you may know and believe that the Father is in Me, and I in Him"* (John 10:38). That has been the nature and heart of God from day one. But it was never fully realized until Jesus.

2. Jesus was a manifestation of the name of the Father. Names reveal nature and identity. Jesus revealed the nature and identity of the Father. He lived in complete harmony with the name of the Father, confessing that He came in His name. (See John 5:43.) The miracles that Jesus performs are done in His Father's name. (See John 10:25.) The right and authority to become children of God was given to those who believe in His name, as He came in the name of His Father. (See John 1:12.)

3. Jesus gave people the word of the Father. Jesus was revealed as the Word of God. (See John 1:1.) He was described as the Word made flesh. (See John 1:14.) He only said what the Father was saying. He also said that those who hear His word and believe have eternal life. (See John 5:24.) Jesus then identifies the source of the word He spoke: *"If anyone loves Me, he will keep My word; and My Father will love him, and We will come to him and make Our home with him. He who does not love Me does not keep My words; and the word which you hear is not Mine but the Father's who sent Me"* (John 14:23–24). Remember that the worlds were created by the word of God. Whenever He spoke, things were created. It's the same today.

Saying what God is saying is one of the things we can do to release His life, love, and Presence into the world around us.

4. Jesus declared His name. He already mentioned that He manifested His name. But now Jesus emphasizes that the name of the Father was also something that had to be declared. Some things must be proclaimed to have full effect. Jesus is the declaration from Heaven as to who this Father is—He is exactly like Jesus! Page after page of the Gospels we see Jesus declaring that all He said and did came from His Father. He took none of the glory for Himself, but instead made it known that He was merely declaring what had to be said.

QUESTIONS FOR REFLECTION: READ JOHN 17

Write down your understanding of each assignment of Jesus, based on John 17.

1.   I have finished the work (verse 4).

_____

_____

_____

_____

_____

_____

_____

_____

2.   I have manifested Your name (verse 6).

_____

_____

_____

_____

_____

_____

_____

3.   I have given them Your word (verse 14).

4.   I have declared Your name (verse 26).

REFLECTION

Every revelation that Jesus unveils about God is an invitation for you to experientially know this same Father.

JESUS SPOKE TO THE STORMS

Then He arose and rebuked the wind, and said to the sea, "Peace, be still!" And the wind ceased and there was a great calm.
—MARK 4:39

Jesus healed all who came to Him, no exceptions. He also healed all the Father directed Him to heal. Setting another standard than what Jesus gave us is unacceptable.

Jesus stilled every life-threatening storm that He encountered. We never see Him using His authority to increase the impact of a storm or to bring calamity of any kind. Never once did He command the storm to destroy a city so that its citizens would become more humble and learn to pray, thus becoming more like Him. Today, many of our spiritual leaders announce why God sent the storm—to break the pride and sinfulness of a region. Obviously God can use any tragedy to His purposes. But that doesn't mean the problem was His design. Jesus didn't deal with storms in that way. Regardless of how or why the storm came about, Jesus was the solution. In our world many insurance companies and newspapers call natural disasters "acts of God." Perhaps they got their theology from us.

By thinking that God causes our storms, diseases, and conflicts, are we resorting to the same reasoning as did James and John when they said, *"as Elijah did"*? (See Luke 9:54.) They justified their thinking by using an Old Testament standard for a New Testament dilemma. Are we truly justified for having such a response because we can find a biblical precedent in the Old Testament?

Why did Jesus rebuke the storm instead of just telling it to stop? The implication is that the powers of darkness were involved in the storm, and they needed to be dealt with because they violated the heart and purpose of God on the earth. And if the devil is involved in the storm, we don't want to be found saying the storm is the will of the Father.

QUESTIONS FOR REFLECTION

1. If Jesus spoke "peace" to the storms He faced, what should be your response as one who is called to follow Jesus' example?

_____

_____

_____

_____

_____

_____

_____

2. What is the danger in thinking/believing that God actually causes the storms? What kind of conflict might this thinking introduce into your prayer life?

_____

_____

_____

_____

_____

_____

_____

_____

_____

_____

POINT OF REFLECTION

Jesus did not cause storms; He calmed them. He is the model we are called to follow, which means that we are to speak peace and stillness to the storms that come across our paths. Jesus is the definitive model for how we are supposed to respond to the problems, chaos. and storms of life that attempt to prevent the good purposes of God from being displayed.

Jesus Healed Everyone Who Came to Him

For this purpose the Son of God was manifested, that
He might destroy the works of the devil.
—1 John 3:8

Two thousand years ago, all sickness was considered to be from the devil, and healing was from God—a sign of the present reality of God's Kingdom. Even something as simple as a fever was considered to be of the devil (see Mark 1:31). Things have disintegrated so far that many consider sickness to be sent or allowed by God to build our character, while those who pursue the ministry of healing are thought to be out of balance at best, and from the devil at worst. This is especially true if that person believes that everyone is to be healed. It's frightening to see how far things can fall in two thousand years. What is even more puzzling is that the very ones who consider the sickness to be approved or even sent by God for our benefit have no problem going to the doctor to find a cure and release from disease. Such mindless approaches to Scripture must stop. And those who would never receive prayer for healing consider going to the doctor *common sense*. It may be *common*, but it lacks *sense* when it violates the example given to us in Scripture. Sometimes when we lack the experience mentioned in Scripture, we tend to look for an obscure passage that somehow explains and/or excuses our lack of experience in the place of the overwhelming evidence given through the life of Jesus.

For what it's worth, I have no problem with going to doctors or taking medicine. They can be used by God to bring about the intended result—health. You just can't have it both ways—believe that God sent a disease to teach us and then try to get rid of it through medical intervention. If that is your belief, you are violating the sovereignty of God. I do have a concern that so many live under the influence of "modern medicine" and give little or no thought to going to the Great Physician. I pray for healing but am willing to accept medical assistance, and I personally do that without shame.

It astounds me that the effort to be like Jesus can be so controversial. And strangely the opposition comes from those who confess Christ. In this day when people say we're to become Christlike, they mean that we're to be patient, kind, loving, etc. The purity part of life is essential to being a faithful witness. But the power aspect is equal in importance. Purity and power are the two legs we stand on in giving witness to the resurrection of Jesus Christ, which is what we are witnesses of—the resurrection.

QUESTIONS FOR REFLECTION

1. What does Jesus reveal about the Father's will for physical healing?

_____

_____

_____

_____

_____

_____

_____

_____

_____

2. Explain how both purity and power are both needed to accurately represent Jesus.

_____

_____

_____

_____

_____

_____

_____

_____

_____

POINT OF REFLECTION

When you read the Gospels, it's clear that Jesus healed every person who came to Him to receive healing. This reveals that God the Father desires to heal the sick. Even though this has become somewhat of a controversial practice in recent centuries, the original standard was that healing, signs, and wonders were regarded as essential, visible demonstrations that the Kingdom of God had come in power. Previous generations should not be our example or benchmark for walking in God's resurrection power; the Master's design should be, as revealed by the very Son of God Himself.

GOD'S GOODNESS DEMONSTRATED THROUGH HIS PERFECT WILL

The will of God has been a much-debated subject, which I often find quite entertaining. It does us no good to keep the conversation in a classroom caught up in Christian theory. It has to be taken onto the streets, where the hurting people are.

NOTES ON SESSION 7

Sometimes we're asking for answers when what we need is Presence.

> *God works in mysterious ways, but He is mysteriously good—not mysteriously evil.*

> *We cannot create a Christian life that is okay with no breakthrough.*

DISCUSSION QUESTIONS

1. What do we typically use as our standard for life (instead of the blueprint pictured in Isaiah 9:7 of an ever-increasing Kingdom)?

2. Why have people come to the conclusion: Revival happens for a season? What is often used as the template for evaluating and defining revival?

3. Describe the two expressions of God's will that Pastor Bill talks about.

   a. Explain the "fixed" will of God—what are some examples of this?

   b. Explain the "desire" or dream of God—what are some examples of this?

4. Explain the comment: "Sometimes we're looking for answers when what we need is Presence."

5. How is "on earth as it is in Heaven" an expression of God's will? What role do we have in seeing this fulfilled?

6. Explain the difference between God being in charge and in control. Is it possible for God to be in charge, but not be in control?

7. How should we respond to shame and guilt when things don't happen according to the way we were praying?

8. Consider Mark 9:14–29. When you don't experience breakthrough or results—just like the disciples did in this passage—what should you do? What model did they set?

ACTIVATION EXERCISE: TAKE JESUS ASIDE...

The goal of today's session was to help you biblically reconsider the subject of God's will. Just because something happens in your life or in the world does not mean, by default, it is God's will. While there are fixed, definitive expressions of God's will—like the return of Jesus—there is a realm of God's will where He invites His people to participate in its unfolding. This does not undermine His sovereignty, as the Sovereign Lord intentionally commissioned mankind to rule in His stead on the earth. This was established in Genesis, at the creation of mankind, and was restored through the work of Jesus when He reclaimed the keys of authority. Your commission is to go into all the world, make disciples of nations, and proclaim the Gospel of the Kingdom. Even though we fail at this assignment, our failure does not revoke God's assignment. When we don't see breakthrough and results, we need to approach the Father—not in guilt or shame—but in a genuine hunger to see an increase of His power, rule, and reign through our lives.

FAITH IN ACTION: ASK FOR HEAVEN'S STRATEGY FOR BREAKTHROUGH

Divide into small groups of prayer partners. Here is the mission: go into God's Presence and, like the disciples, take Jesus aside.

- Ask God your hard questions; don't blame Him, but learn how to ask Him, and ask Him honestly.

- Ask your prayer partners to pray for you, and likewise pray for them. Pray for perseverance to keep praying and believing God. Pray for strength. Pray for healing, specifically for disappointment and loss. Release freedom from any guilt or shame. Simply release God's refreshing Presence over every person.

- Continue praying in small groups, or you can come back together as a large group.

- Collect prayer requests—specifically, requests that have gone "unanswered" for a long period of time. This is your prayer assignment today. Focus on praying for personal breakthroughs, healings, lost family members, relationship restoration, deliverance from torment, freedom from addiction, etc. Keep praying and keep believing, regardless of how dark the situation is or has become.

RECOGNIZE WHAT YOU HAVE BEEN GIVEN

Freely you have received, freely give.
—MATTHEW 10:8

I can die of starvation with a million dollars in the bank. If I don't make withdrawals from what's in my account, my wealth is no better than a dream, principle, or fantasy. Everything in our account in Christ is beyond our wildest dreams. We can't make a withdrawal if we don't know what exists. Jesus models the mere beginning of what's in our account. The promises of His Word give us even greater insight into this superior reality. It's time to see what Jesus has so we can see what Jesus gave us. Here's the bottom line—He gave us everything that belongs to Him. And the Father gave Him everything! Look at it here in John 16:14–15, speaking of the work of the Holy Spirit—*"He will glorify Me, for He will take of what is Mine and declare it to you. All things that the Father has are Mine. Therefore I said that He will take of Mine and declare it to you."*

This really is an amazing passage of Scripture, one for which we bear great responsibility. The Holy Spirit releases what Jesus alone possesses into our accounts through declaration. Every time He speaks to us, He transfers the eternal resources of Jesus to our account, enabling us to complete our assignment: *"Heal the sick, cleanse the lepers, raise the dead, cast out demons. Freely you have received, freely give. …Go therefore and make disciples of all the nations, baptizing them in the name of the Father and of the Son and of the Holy Spirit, teaching them to observe all things that I have commanded you; and lo, I am with you always, even to the end of the age"* (Matt. 10:8; 28:19-20). Notice it says for the disciples to teach their converts all that Jesus taught them. That *must* include the instruction to heal the sick, cast out devils, etc. There was never to be a discrepancy between how we live today and His initial standard.

When Jesus worked in miracles, was He merely creating an appetite in us to be in Heaven for eternity? Heaven should always remain something we are passionate about. It was Jesus who taught us how to pray, *"On earth as it is in heaven"* (Matt. 6:10). Yes, eternity is important. But going to Heaven is not my responsibility. He will get me there, entirely by His grace. My job is very specific and extremely important—bring Heaven to earth through prayer and obedience. Please notice that when Jesus declared the Kingdom was at hand, He displayed it by giving life, breaking the powers of darkness, and restoring broken lives, hearts, and homes. He told us to pick up the same message. Why should we expect a different outcome?

QUESTIONS FOR REFLECTION

1. Explain what it means to make a "withdrawal" from your spiritual bank account.

_____

_____

_____

_____

_____

_____

_____

_____

_____

_____

_____

_____

_____

2. Reflection on Matthew 10:8: Describe what it looks like to make withdrawals from this account; what do you think is the key to seeing and experiencing more of God's power released through your life?

_____

_____

_____

_____

_____

_____

_____

3. How does Matthew 6:10, on earth as it is in Heaven, give you a standard for what God's will is supposed to look like? How is this your assignment?

PRAYER OF SURRENDER

Holy Spirit, thank You for Your Presence in my life.

You have equipped me with all of the resources and all of the power to carry out Jesus' mandate "on earth as it is in Heaven."

This is my assignment, and I joyfully accept it.

I trust You, Father, to get me to Heaven. That was paid for by the blood of Jesus.

I will get there completely by Your grace, and I trust You with the process.

While I am here on earth, show me what it looks like to be an ambassador of Your Kingdom.

Use my life to reveal Your will to a world that wonders what You're looking like.

Two Dimensions of God's Will

Your kingdom come. Your will be done on earth as it is in heaven.
—MATTHEW 6:10

The great Bible teacher Bob Mumford wrote a wonderful book entitled *The King and You*. It was here I learned something about the will of God that has helped me immensely. There are two different words used in the original language of the New Testament for the word *will*, as it is used throughout Scripture. One is *boulema*; the other is *thelema*. *Boulema* means "the eternal counsels of God which are unfolding through the ages—His purpose—His determination." It is going to be done whether you and I like it or not. God's intention will come to pass. However, *thelema*, which means "God's wish or desire," most often depends upon the response of each individual for fulfillment.

This is huge. God has desires that may or may not be fulfilled. Make no mistake. He has the power to make anything happen that He wants to happen. But He has the heart to work with the process of the development of His people to take responsibility and co-labor with Him. The outcome of this process is we become a people who look and live like His Son, Jesus.

The first word for the will of God, *boulema*, that I mentioned above is referring to things that are unchangeable. For example, Jesus is coming back. You can vote *yes*, *no*, or *I don't care*. It matters not. We don't have a role in that decision. It is put entirely in the hands of the Father, who alone determines how and when that event will happen. On the other hand, there are many things that God would like to have happen, and has made possible, but they never will be, because believers either don't believe they are the will of God anymore or are waiting for God Himself to do them. That will is represented with the word *thelema*. I remind you of the time Jesus told the disciples to feed the multitude of thousands when they had nothing but a child's lunch. Jesus never took back His commission to do it Himself when they said they were unable to accomplish that impossible task. He still set the stage for them to see the miracle through their hands as they handed out the food. And they did. (See Mark 6:37–44.)

The will of God has been a much-debated subject, which I often find quite entertaining. It does us no good to keep the conversation in a classroom caught up in Christian theory. It has to be taken onto the streets, where the hurting people are. The will of God must be displayed by a praying people, unwilling to sit on the sidelines and see the devil continually steal, kill, and destroy, and then watch the theorist give God the credit. Masking our unbelief with a spineless theology is the great deception. This continual misrepresentation of the nature and heart of God for one another and for the world must stop. Stupidity often looks like intelligence in the absence of experience.

QUESTIONS FOR REFLECTION

1. Explain your understanding of the two expressions of God's will outlined in this daily reading:

    a. *Boulema*

    _____

    _____

    _____

    _____

    _____

    _____

    _____

    _____

    _____

    _____

    b. *Thelema*

    _____

    _____

    _____

    _____

    _____

    _____

    _____

    _____

    _____

    _____

    _____

    _____

2. Explain how it's possible for God to have a will that is actually unfulfilled. How does He invite people into the fulfillment of His will?

_____

_____

_____

_____

_____

_____

_____

_____

_____

_____

_____

_____

_____

_____

_____

PRAYER OF CONSECRATION

Father in Heaven, I praise You.

I honor and awe Your Name.

Your Name is holy.

You are God in Heaven and I worship You.

I say "Yes" to the charge to see Your Kingdom come, Your rule and reign advanced, on earth as it is in Heaven.

Show me how to think from Heaven's perspective so I can release Heaven's solutions.

Help me to see and live from Heaven to earth, so that earth can look more like Heaven.

And Your dream, God, is fulfilled.

Your dream of seeing the nations receive Your Son and experience the transformation You've made available.

Start with me, Lord.

Right here, right where You've positioned me.

Day Thirty-Three

GOD IS IN CHARGE...NOT IN CONTROL

And we know that all things work together for good to those who love
God, to those who are the called according to His purpose.
—ROMANS 8:28

One of the most common phrases used in this discussion is that "God is in control." It is true that He is the Sovereign God. He reigns over all, and everything belongs to Him. Nothing is outside of His reach or His concern. He is all-knowing and all-powerful. But is He in control?

This is not a question of His ability or His power and authority. If He is, doesn't that make Him responsible for Hitler? Is brain cancer His idea? If He is in control, then we have to credit Him with disease, earthquakes, hurricanes, and all the other calamities in life. You get the point. I think it's more accurate to say He is in charge, but He is not in control. Every parent reading this should get this point quite easily. While we are in charge of our homes, not everything that happens under our roof is necessarily our idea or is approved by us. This is an important distinction.

God can work any situation around for His glory. He is that good. And I'm thankful. I've witnessed the most horrific things happen to people, and I've seen them turn to this Father of grace and have watched as God has healed their hearts to a place of unexplainable strength. But to credit Him as the cause of the problem because He can use it redemptively is illogical and foolish. It violates the nature of God revealed in Jesus Christ. The fruit of such confusion within the family about the nature of our Father is a world around us that is even more confused about the nature of this God we have claimed wants to save them.

QUESTIONS FOR REFLECTION

1. Based on the video session you watched this week and your daily reading, explain the difference between God being in charge and in control.

_____

_____

_____

_____

_____

_____

_____

_____

2. Why is it so important that you recognize the difference between God directly causing a problem and God working that situation for His glory (without causing it)?

_____

_____

_____

_____

_____

_____

_____

_____

_____

_____

_____

_____

PRAYER OF DISCERNMENT

God, help me to rightly divide between what is Your will and what is not.
Help me to discern the difference between what You cause and what the enemy causes.
I know You work all things together for good.
But just because you work things together doesn't mean You directly caused them.
Thank You for being good, all the time.
There is no shadow of turning in You.
Yes, there are things You do that are mysterious, and I don't understand them.
But You are always mysteriously good!

THE DESIRES AND DREAMS OF GOD

He (God) is restraining himself on account of you, holding back the End because he doesn't want anyone lost. He's giving everyone space and time to change.
—2 PETER 3:9 MSG

God has desires, wishes, and dreams. He brought us into a relationship with Him as a part of that dream. None of us were forced into this relationship with God. Now we have a position in Christ to help bring about more of His desire by having influence on what happens and what doesn't happen on planet Earth. For example, consider this very simple illustration. We carry the message of salvation. This message must be preached in all the world. If we send preachers of this message to one nation, but refuse to send any to another, there will be many times the amount of converts in the nation we chose to serve with the Gospel. Does it mean that God willed the others to miss out on eternal life? No. We did. That was our choice.

God is *"not willing that any should perish but that all should come to repentance"* (2 Pet. 3:9). What is God's will in this passage? That no one would perish in their sins, but that *all* would come to repentance. That is the will of God. Is it happening? No. Is it His fault? No. Does that mean that He is lacking the ability to bring about His desire? No. He made it possible for all to come to Christ. He gave us an example to follow in Jesus. He made us sinless through the blood of Jesus. He then commissioned us by Jesus. Then He empowered us with the same power that Jesus had in His earthly ministry. He made it possible for the will of God to be done on earth as it is in Heaven. The catalyst of that becoming reality is a people who pray—relentlessly pray—what He told us to pray: *"on earth as it is in heaven"* (Matt. 6:10).

QUESTIONS FOR REFLECTION

1.   What should the "dream of God" or "desire of God" statements in Scripture do to you? How should you receive them as invitations to pray?

_____
_____
_____
_____
_____
_____
_____
_____
_____
_____

2. Review and reflect on Second Peter 3:9. What does this passage say about the desires and dreams of God (beyond that He wants everyone to repent and receive salvation)?

_____
_____
_____
_____
_____
_____
_____
_____
_____
_____

INVITATION FOR PRAYER

God is inviting you to partner with His dreams and desires. While there are certain aspects of His will that are absolutely fixed and not subject to mankind's participation, Scripture makes it clear that there are also desires of God that come to fruition (or don't) because of human involvement. Use this truth as your charge to boldly pray and take risks. Many have given up on the dreams of God because of what they don't see; don't let this be your approach. Let what you see in the Scripture be more real than what you see with your natural eyes. Let the dreams of God deeply compel you to pray for transformed nations, massive global revival, and the outpouring of His Spirit to touch all flesh.

Day Thirty-Five

YOUR SUMMONS TO "GO"

Now there is in Jerusalem by the Sheep Gate a pool, which is called in Hebrew,
Bethesda, having five porches. In these lay a great multitude of sick people,
blind, lame, paralyzed, waiting for the moving of the water. For an angel went
down at a certain time into the pool and stirred up the water; then whoever
stepped in first, after the stirring of the water, was made well of whatever
disease he had. Now a certain man was there who had an infirmity thirty-
eight years. When Jesus saw him lying there, and knew that he already
had been in that condition a long time, He said to him, "Do you want to be
made well?" The sick man answered Him, "Sir, I have no man to put me
into the pool when the water is stirred up; but while I am coming, another
steps down before me." Jesus said to him, "Rise, take up your bed and walk."
And immediately the man was made well, took up his bed, and walked.
—JOHN 5:2–9

This is such a beautiful story of a man without hope being touched by the compassion of Jesus. Jesus came to him representing the heavenly Father. It's priceless. If this story were to happen today, there would be initial excitement by some. But the newspaper columnists, the TV anchors, the theologians, pastors, and teachers would be interviewing the people that were around the pool that weren't healed. I'm told there easily could have been up to one thousand people or more gathered around that pool, hoping for their chance at a miracle by getting into the pool after the angel stirred the water. The interview would go something like this: "How did it feel to have Jesus walk past you to heal someone else?" Some would use that platform to warn people of the danger of getting their hopes up, as the camera sweeps across the crowd of lame and diseased people. Many of those who represent the Church would then come to the conclusion that while this one act may have been from God, it is rather obvious evidence that it is not God's will to heal everyone. Why? Instead of trying to show us what God could do, He was trying to show us what one man could do who had no sin and was completely empowered by the Holy Spirit. If we're that concerned about this pool surrounded by sick people, *Go! "Go into all the world"* (Mark 16:15).

This will of God is not complicated. Jesus is the will of God. He points to a perfect Father. And that Father has great dreams and desires for each of us. We are in His heart of dreams. And those dreams are for both now and eternity. Taking the time to consider Him and think according to His heart and His nature will have a dramatic effect on what we see and experience during our lifetime. We owe it to everyone around us to consider Him as He is—a good and perfect Father.

QUESTIONS FOR REFLECTION

1. Reflect on John 5:2–9. How does this gospel account give you a glimpse of what you have been called to do and the audience you have been called to impact?

2. How does this story reveal what God the Father is like through the example of Jesus?

_____

_____

_____

_____

_____

_____

_____

_____

_____

_____

_____

_____

_____

_____

_____

_____

_____

_____

_____

PRAYER OF EMPOWERMENT

Holy Spirit, I ask You to come again and fill me to overflowing.

Help me to see those who are hurting around me and bring Your healing Presence to them.

Open my eyes to those in my own world—family, friends, and co-workers—who need a touch from a good God.

Show me how I can participate in Your will for their lives and see Your desires for them come to pass.

Thank You, Lord, for Your empowerment!

GOD'S GOODNESS IS AN ANCHOR IN MYSTERY, TRAGEDY, AND DISAPPOINTMENT

It is not the task of Christianity to provide easy answers to every question, but to make us progressively aware of a mystery. God is not so much the object of our knowledge as the cause of our wonder.
—KALLISTOS WARE

NOTES ON SESSION 8

Bold faith stands on the shoulders of quiet trust.

_____

_____

_____

_____

_____

_____

_____

_____

_____

_____

_____

_____

_____

_____

_____

_____

_____

_____

_____

When God restores, He restores to a place greater than before.

_____

_____

_____

_____

_____

_____

_____

_____

_____

_____

_____

DISCUSSION QUESTIONS

1. Discuss the following quote:

    *It is not the task of Christianity to provide easy answers to every
    question, but to make us progressively aware of a mystery. God is not
    so much the object of our knowledge as the cause of our wonder.*
    —KALLISTOS WARE

    a. Explain the connection between people coming up with "bad theology" and how they respond to mystery.

2. What does it mean that bold faith stands on the shoulders of quiet trust?

3. Read Romans 8:28. Explain how this passage of Scripture is an anchor during mystery (when prayers don't get instantly answered or we experience disappointment).

4. Explain the difference between Matthew 11:12 (the violence of faith) and Mark 10:15 (receiving a gift as a child).

    a. Discuss how you can know when to "rest" as a child or engage in the violent act of faith.

5. Discuss why it's not helpful to ask God why? In these times, what do you need most from God? (It's not necessarily answers that can be grasped by the mind.)

6. Discuss the difference between healthy mourning and unhealthy mourning. How should mourning and loss drive you into the Presence of God?

7. Read Proverbs 6:30-31. Discuss what it means to pray for vindication using this Scripture as a reference point.

8. How can the vindication of God released in your life actually reveal His goodness to the people around you?

ACTIVATION EXERCISE: RESPONDING TO THE MYSTERY

In this session, Pastor Bill walks viewers through some of the undiscussed facts concerning loss, disappointment, and mystery. There is an appropriate response to mystery, which results from loss. It's not to live in extended mourning, nor is it right to reject mourning and pretend everything is okay. It's healthy to mourn in such a way that we are drawn into God's Presence, receive His loving touch, and then emerge from that season with an expectation of vindication. It's not vindication to fulfill a longing for personal revenge, but more so a desire that the goodness of God would be made visible on our lives because of His restorative touch on every area that experienced loss.

FAITH IN ACTION: ASK FOR HEAVEN'S VINDICATION AND INCREASED ANOINTING

This will be a time of corporate prayer. If you sense the Holy Spirit directing, you can transition from the time of group prayer into prayer partners or individual prayer. This is a very sensitive time, particularly for those who have experienced any measure of loss for which there is mystery in their lives.

Remind yourself of the assurance of Romans 8:28 and that God's summons is not to act like we've never experienced tragedy, but more to respond to it correctly.

Prayer directions:

- Pray for a healing mourning period for every person who has experienced loss—where they can go into God's Presence and share their heart with Him. Receive His love rather than trying to get all of your questions answered.

- Pray for a discernment of seasons—so that people are not ensnared by extended mourning, but recognize the healthy time to mourn and the time to transition.

- Pray for a revelation of vindication—that those who have experienced loss and tragedy would see their mystery as an invitation to vindication. What produced mystery in your life is actually the very target you are being called to pursue in prayer with an expectation of increased breakthrough. It's not about reacting to the thief who stole (the devil), but it's about living in response to the Father who wants to show His goodness in an extreme way.

- Pray for recompense and restoration on the basis of Proverbs 6:30-31. Declare and announce restoration over everything that has been lost, as the Lord makes all things new.

- Pray for an anointing over those who experienced loss. Declare that this anointing, released through your life, would destroy the very things that caused loss, tragedy, and disappointment.

- Pray for the demonstration of God's goodness in unusual ways as people see God's vindication releasing restoration and anointing in your life.

EMBRACING MYSTERY AND TRUST

It is not the task of Christianity to provide easy answers to every question, but to make us progressively aware of a mystery. God is not so much the object of our knowledge as the cause of our wonder.
—KALLISTOS WARE

This quote from Kallistos Ware is one of the most meaningful quotes I have read in many years. God is more than capable of going head to head with anyone in debate. The thought that God might be intimidated with humanity's questions is quite humorous. He invites us into this dialogue. (See Isaiah 1:18.) It's just that He has a different value system than we do, although ours is changing daily in our walk with Him. And to have a relationship with Him is always on His terms. But we know that His terms are always for our best. God has one basic requirement of anyone who approaches Him—faith. *"Without faith it is impossible to please Him"* (Heb. 11:6). That is what He values.

Living in the place of trust positions us for breakthroughs—bold faith stands on the shoulders of quiet trust. Faith is an activity of the heart. Real faith comes through yieldedness, not some trumped-up activity of the brain. Faith comes from surrender, not striving. Faith is not mindless. Understanding with the renewed mind (see Rom. 12:2) can often be used to set the context for faith to work in, much like the banks of a river set the parameters for the flow of the water. While faith is not mindless, it is also not mind-full. It is not intellectual in nature. True faith is superior to reason in that it gives our intellect a context in which to grow safely—in the knowledge of God. Remember, it's the fool who says in His heart there is no God. (See Psalm 14:1; 53:1.) The Eternal God is the cornerstone of all logic and reason.

QUESTIONS FOR REFLECTION

1. Why do you think that asking for answers from God might not be the correct response to tragedy, loss, or disappointment?

_____

_____

_____

_____

_____

_____

_____

_____

_____

_____

_____

_____

2.   Explain why what you need most in the midst of mystery is not answers but trusting in God's Presence.

_____

_____

_____

_____

_____

_____

_____

_____

_____

_____

_____

_____

_____

REMINDER

Living in the place of trust positions us for breakthroughs—bold faith stands on the shoulders of quiet trust.

Day Thirty-Seven

Not with the Head, but with the Heart

To know the love of Christ which passes knowledge; that
you may be filled with all the fullness of God.
—Ephesians 3:19

God cannot be comprehended. If it were possible, we, not He, would be God—the finite will never envelop the infinite. He is to be known by relationship. Consider the wonder of the Almighty God even wanting for us to know Him. Because Jesus took our sins upon Himself, we are authorized to approach the Father with the same qualifications that Jesus has in coming before His Father. Jesus is received and celebrated by a perfect Father who is always good. Every true believer is equally received and celebrated because we are in Christ.

To know God is the greatest privilege given to anyone. The cross of Jesus Christ is the ultimate invitation to know God. It is here we can know with certainty He has spared no expense in enabling us to respond successfully to His invitation.

Clarity on this mystery of head vs. heart is given in Ephesians 3:19. It says, *"to know the love of Christ which passes knowledge; that you may be filled with all the fullness of God."* The word *know* is a word that means "knowledge gained through experience." It is experiential knowledge. The word *knowledge* means "to comprehend." In so many words Paul is saying, *that we might know the love of God by experience in a way we could never comprehend or fully understand.* It's not that knowledge is wrong, or that ignorance is exalted. Knowledge is vital. We have teachers in the Body of Christ so we will learn. In fact, one of the main responsibilities of the Holy Spirit is to teach us—it's a divine priority. But we must require of our own hearts that the knowledge of Him takes us to Him. Through an encounter with God, we grow in divine wisdom. It's that knowledge is not required for faith.

QUESTIONS FOR REFLECTION

1. Describe the difference between responding to mystery with your "head" or "heart."

_____
_____
_____
_____
_____
_____
_____
_____
_____
_____
_____

2.   What does experiential knowledge of God look like?

_____
_____
_____
_____
_____
_____
_____
_____
_____
_____
_____
_____
_____
_____

REMINDER

God cannot be comprehended. If it were possible, we, not He, would be God. The finite will never envelop the infinite. He is to be known by relationship.

Your Invitation for Vindication

*People do not despise a thief if he steals to satisfy himself when
he is starving. Yet when he is found, he must restore sevenfold;
he may have to give up all the substance of his house.*
—PROVERBS 6:30-31

I had a conversation with Rick Joyner on the phone a couple of days before my dad's death. He told me that this loss would give me access to a seven times greater anointing against this particular disease. That may sound a bit awkward to some, but I knew of the principle first established by Solomon in the Proverbs passage above.

The devil is called the thief, and he stole from our family when my father died of pancreatic cancer. I also knew that greater anointing was not to be given automatically. It would require time in the *secret place*, crying out for the more that God had promised. It was not begging, in the sense of there being a fear God wouldn't keep His promise. I just knew that not everything was automatic. Sometimes He waits to see if the promise will awaken something in us that can carry the weightiness of the answer we've asked for. When answers to prayer come to a yielded heart, they release greater strength. But when answers come to a resistant heart, they carry a high probability of deepening the independence that causes conflict with God in the first place. The recalibration of our value system needed to be consistent with His.

The Book of First Samuel has a story that becomes vital for us in this journey. There is a woman named Hannah, who was barren. And while she was loved much by her husband, she was not fulfilled in life without a child. At the same time, we find Israel was in trouble again, and God desired a solution—He wanted them to have a trustworthy prophet. Hannah became so desperate in her prayers that she promised God that if He would bless her with a son, she would return the child to God, dedicating him to a life of ministry. Without knowing it, she aligned her heart's cry for a son with God's heart cry for a prophet. It was when both worlds came into agreement that we see Heaven invade earth, giving her the son she longed for. She went on to have many more children, as God honored her sacrifice of heart to meet the longing He had for Israel to have a trusted voice from God.

I do believe God hates cancer and that He wants His people to rise up with His hatred toward that disease. But hate it enough to seek God in private and take risk in public. As I've stated before, there are times when our love for God can be measured by what we hate. And in this case, hate what He hates—disease.

How do you think our perfect Father feels about sickness and disease? It was the burden of all of humanity's afflictions for all time that was put upon His Son, Jesus Christ. He bore our sickness upon His body in His suffering so we could be healed. How should a Father feel toward a disease that has such a painful impact on His Son? That is how we are to feel. We must hate what He hates and love what He loves.

QUESTIONS FOR REFLECTION

1. Based on Proverbs 6:30-31, what expectation should you have about loss and being robbed by the enemy?

_____

_____

_____

_____

_____

_____

_____

_____

_____

_____

2. How should you respond to the invitation of loss and pain? (Consider Hannah in First Samuel, based on today's daily reading.)

_____

_____

_____

_____

_____

_____

3. Pray and ask the Holy Spirit to bring to your remembrance areas where you've experienced loss and disappointment. You might not need to think/pray about this too quickly. Now, ask the Lord how you can partner with God to receive promise of vindication.

4. Write down what the Holy Spirit shows you/shares with you in the lined space below.

REMINDER

Sometimes God waits to see if His promises will awaken something in us that can carry the weightiness of the answers we've asked for.

TRUSTING IN THE TRIAL

Trust in the Lord with all your heart; do not depend on your own understanding.
—PROVERBS 3:5 NLT

The need for mystery need not be painful or dreaded. It is a part of our ongoing story. We value the outcome—the miracles, the breakthroughs, and the divine interventions—as we should. But He seems to treasure the process—that which takes us to the outcome. It's the process that reveals and demonstrates our devotion to Him. Devotion, that realm of established trust, is something He can build upon. God is the ultimate entrepreneur, building the unexpected in the earth upon and through the lives of His trusted saints.

What we really believe about Him becomes evident in trial. Answers to prayers are the easiest things in the world for God. He is all-powerful. What He doesn't control is our response to Him. He has influence, but not control, as He has given us a most valuable gift—a free will. When our will is surrendered to His purposes, all of creation gets closer to the healing God promised, as His people find out who they are. (See Romans 8:19.) We are to reign with Christ. It's vital to see this destiny in the way it was presented to us, as our beloved King put a towel over His arm and washed His disciples' feet. He rules to serve. Our privilege in life is to serve with the heart of a king and rule with the heart of a servant. Reigning with Christ will never equip us to exercise power over people but instead will allow us the opportunity to serve sacrificially—following the example given to us by Jesus.

QUESTIONS FOR REFLECTION

1. How does trusting God during trials reveal our devotion to Him?

_____

_____

_____

_____

_____

_____

_____

_____

_____

_____

_____

_____

_____

_____

_____

_____

_____

2. Reflect on Proverbs 3:5. How can your own understanding interfere with you trusting in the Lord? What do you think the key is to trusting Him and not being distracted by the different thoughts/ explanations that are bombarding you?

_____

_____

_____

_____

_____

_____

_____

_____

_____

_____

_____

_____

_____

_____

3. What area(s) do you need to trust God in right now? Ask the Holy Spirit to help you trust the Lord without leaning on your own understanding. Ask Him to give you promises from Scripture to anchor your heart in. Ask Him to wash your mind in the water of His word (see Eph. 5:26) so that your thinking is in agreement with His thinking.

REMINDER

God is the ultimate entrepreneur, building the unexpected in the earth upon and through the lives of His trusted saints.

ALL THINGS WORK TOGETHER FOR GOOD

The secret things belong to the Lord our God, but those things which are revealed belong to us and to our children forever, that we may do all the words of this law.
—DEUTERONOMY 29:29

It's wisdom to realize what God has given us access to and what is to remain entirely in His possession. This is where trust is proven.

I believe in miracles and have seen more than I ever even hoped to see as a young man. My experience has been what Jesus promised—the blind see, the deaf hear, the lame walk, and the poor have the Good News declared to them. My conclusion is miracles happen entirely by His grace. I've seen them happen when there was great faith, as well as when there was simple obedience in prayer but no real expectation of a miracle. It's still all by grace. And while this life of following Jesus is to be a life filled with supernatural interventions, we are given the following passage for a reason: *"And we know that all things work together for good to those who love God, to those who are the called according to His purpose"* (Rom. 8:28).

Such a promise would never be necessary if everything worked the way we expected. God is not a vending machine where we put in a coin and pull the handle and get what we requested. He is a Father that is to be known. Trusting Him enough to embrace mystery as a gift is one of the quickest ways to come to know this One who is beyond knowing, whose ways are always good.

QUESTIONS FOR REFLECTION

1. Reflect on Deuteronomy 29:29. How does this passage of Scripture protect you from trying to get answers that God might not be sharing?

_____

_____

_____

_____

_____
_____
_____
_____
_____
_____
_____
_____

2. Why is Romans 8:28 such a cornerstone verse when experiencing mystery?

_____
_____
_____
_____
_____
_____
_____
_____
_____

3. For the losses and disappointments you have personally experienced, how would the vindication of God in your life display His goodness?

_____
_____
_____
_____
_____
_____
_____
_____

CLOSING PRAYER

God is Good!

I declare it.

I believe it.

In every season and circumstance, I know that You are good.

I may have unanswered questions.

There may be mystery I'm facing.

Even though I don't have all the answers, I have the greatest answer.

You are a good Father.

I can trust You because You are faithful.

You are the Lord and You do not change.

Even though seasons change.

Circumstances change.

People change.

You are the same—yesterday, today, and forever.

Thank You, Jesus, for showing me what the Father is like.

You revealed Good who is truly good.

Establish it in my heart.

Settle it in my mind.

And above all, let the revelation of Your goodness consume my life and invite others to taste and see it for themselves!

ABOUT BILL JOHNSON

Bill Johnson is a fifth-generation pastor with a rich heritage in the Holy Spirit. Together Bill and his wife Beni serve a growing number of churches that have partnered for revival. This leadership network has crossed denominational lines, building relationships that enable church leaders to walk successfully in both purity and power. Bill and his wife are the senior leaders of Bethel Church, Redding, California. All three of their children and spouses are involved in full-time ministry. They also have nine wonderful grandchildren.

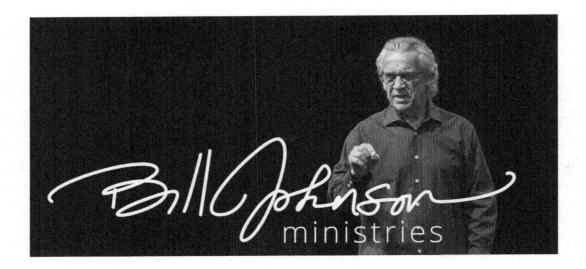

BILL JOHNSON is a fifth-generation pastor with a rich heritage in the movement and works of the Holy Spirit. Bill and his wife, Beni, who are senior leaders of Bethel Church in Redding, California, also serve a growing number of churches that cross denominational lines, exhibit power, and partner together for revival.

The vision of Bill Johnson Ministries is to equip Christ-followers to become Heaven's transformational representatives on Earth - equipping people in all spheres of influence to experience God's presence and operate in His Kingdom power. Bill is also the bestselling author of many books, including *When Heaven Invades Earth*, *Hosting the Presence*, *Supernatural Power of a Transformed Mind* and co-author of *Essential Guide to Healing* with Randy Clark. The Johnsons have three children and nine grandchildren.

OTHER RESOURCES FROM BILL JOHNSON

BOOKS   DEVOTIONALS   TEACHING CURRICULUM & BIBLE STUDIES   CD, DVD, & DIGITAL AUDIO AND VIDEO   MP3 COLLECTIONS

CONNECT WITH PASTOR BILL JOHNSON

website: bjm.org • **media:** Bethel.tv • **resources:** shop.ibethel.org
facebook: facebook.com/BillJohnsonMinistries

FREE E-BOOKS?
YES, PLEASE!

Get **FREE** and deeply-discounted **Christian books** for your **e-reader** delivered to your inbox **every week!**

IT'S SIMPLE!

VISIT lovetoreadclub.com

SUBSCRIBE by entering your email address

RECEIVE free and discounted e-book offers and inspiring articles delivered to your inbox every week!

Unsubscribe at any time.

SUBSCRIBE NOW!

LOVE TO READ CLUB

visit **LOVETOREADCLUB.COM** ▶

Made in the USA
Coppell, TX
26 January 2020